Three Little Words

God's Truth in Simple Terms

TERRY FERGUSON

DISCOVERY HOUSE

PUBLISHERS®

Feeding the Soul with the Word of God

To my child.
I love you
So very much.

Three Little Words: God's Truth in Simple Terms

© 2014 by Terry Ferguson

Discovery House is affiliated with RBC Ministries, Grand Rapids, Michigan.

Requests for permission to quote from this book should be directed to: Permissions Department, Discovery House Publishers, P.O. Box 3566, Grand Rapids, MI 49501, or contact us by e-mail at permissionsdept@dhp.org

Interior design by Melissa Elenbaas

ISBN 978-1-57293-818-2

Printed in the United States of America

First printing in 2014

Introduction

· ·

As a Christian parent, I had long been looking for a way to pass on my love of God's Word to my daughter and to others. One afternoon I was watching television and saw an interview of an old rock-and-roll star. To be honest, I can't even remember who it was, but his answer about what advice he had for his son got my attention. He said, "Put God first, do your best, and just be yourself." I was not expecting the musician to mention God, but was glad that he had done so on national television. I was also impressed that he was prepared, more than I would have been, to give an answer. The third thing that struck me was the simplicity of his advice, which made it easy to remember.

As I thought about his quick, three-word responses, I wondered how many I could come up with that were biblically based. As I jotted down a lengthy list, I thought about how I needed something to make them more than simple platitudes. They needed Scripture to support them and give them substance. The number of verses to use was an easy decision—three—and thus I had a name for my collection, Three Little Words.

The resulting collection is a means to pass on biblical advice to our children or loved ones. It provides a resource for those in need of direction or for those who need a quick pick-me-up from the Word of God. It provides help for both those unfamiliar with God's Word, introducing them to Scripture, and also to the "well-versed" Christian, as simple reminders of God's profound truths. It is my hope that it inspires both the unfamiliar and the familiar to dig deeper into the entirety of God's Word.

The Bible has often been referred to as God's love letter to us. As for my child, and for yours, one of the greatest ways we can show we love them is to introduce them to God's Holy Word. May *Three Little Words* convey to them the underlying message of "I love you" from our heavenly Father and from us earthly parents or friends.

PUT GOD FIRST

God spoke all these words, saying, "I am the Lord your God, who brought you out of the land of Egypt, out of the house of bondage. You shall have no other gods before me."

Exodus 20:1–3

Seek first the kingdom of God and His righteousness, and all these things shall be added to you.

Matthew 6:33 (NKJV)

Jesus answered him, "The first of all the commandments is: 'Hear, O Israel, the Lord our God, the Lord is one. And you shall love the Lord your God with all your heart, with all your soul, with all your mind, and with all your strength.' This is the first commandment.

Mark 12:29–32 (NKJV)

COUNT YOUR BLESSINGS

How precious to me are your thoughts, God! How vast is the sum of them! Were I to count them, they would outnumber the grains of sand—when I awake, I am still with you.

Psalm 139:17–18 (NIV)

Praise be to the God and Father of our Lord Jesus Christ, who has blessed us in the heavenly realms with every spiritual blessing in Christ.

Ephesians 1:3 (NIV)

Thou hast multiplied, O Lord my God, thy wondrous deeds and thy thoughts toward us; none can compare with thee! Were I to proclaim and tell of them, they would be more than can be numbered.

Psalm 40:5

ALWAYS BE PREPARED

In your hearts reverence Christ as Lord. Always be prepared to make a defense to any one who calls you to account for the hope that is in you, yet do it with gentleness and reverence.

1 Peter 3:15

In a great house there are not only vessels of gold and silver, but also of wood and clay, some for honor and some for dishonor. Therefore if anyone cleanses himself from the latter, he will be a vessel for honor, sanctified and useful for the Master, prepared for every good work.

2 Timothy 2:20–21 (NKJV)

Watch therefore, for you know neither the day nor the hour in which the Son of Man is coming.

Matthew 25:13 (NKJV)

YOU ARE GIFTED

There are diversities of gifts, but the same Spirit. There are differences of ministries, but the same Lord. And there are diversities of activities, but it is the same God who works all in all. But the manifestation of the Spirit is given to each one for the profit of all.

1 Corinthians 12:4–7 (NKJV)

By the grace given to me I bid every one among you not to think of himself more highly than he ought to think, but to think with sober judgment . . . For as in one body we have many members, and all the members do not have the same function, so we, though many, are one body in Christ . . . Having gifts that differ according to the grace given to us, let us use them.

Romans 12:3–6

As each one has received a gift, minister it to one another, as good stewards of the manifold grace of God.

1 Peter 4:10 (NKJV)

LOVE ONE ANOTHER

A new commandment I give to you, that you love one another; even as I have loved you, that you also love one another. By this all men will know that you are my disciples, if you have love for one another.

John 13:34–35

Owe no one anything except to love one another, for he who loves another has fulfilled the law.

Romans 13:8 (NKJV)

Now I beg you, lady, not as though I were writing you a new commandment, but the one we have had from the beginning, that we love one another.

2 John 1:5

CAST OFF CARES

Humble yourselves under the mighty hand of God, that He may exalt you in due time, casting all your care upon Him, for He cares for you.

1 Peter 5:6–7 (NKJV)

Do not be anxious about anything, but in every situation, by prayer and petition, with thanksgiving, present your requests to God. And the peace of God, which transcends all understanding, will guard your hearts and your minds in Christ Jesus.

Philippians 4:6–7 (NIV)

Cast your burden on the Lord, and he will sustain you; he will never permit the righteous to be moved.

Psalm 55:22

SEEK WISE COUNSEL

Where there is no counsel, the people fall; but in the multitude of counselors there is safety.

Proverbs 11:14 (NKJV)

Without counsel, plans go awry, but in the multitude of counselors they are established.

Proverbs 15:22 (NKJV)

Blessed is the man who walks not in the counsel of the wicked, nor stands in the way of sinners, nor sits in the seat of scoffers; but his delight is in the law of the Lord, and on his law he meditates day and night.

Psalm 1:1–2

GUARD YOUR REPUTATION

A good name is to be chosen rather than great riches, and favor is better than silver or gold.

Proverbs 22:1

Therefore, brethren, seek out from among you seven men of good reputation, full of the Holy Spirit and wisdom, whom we may appoint over this business.

Acts 6:3 (NKJV)

A good name is better than precious ointment; and the day of death than the day of one's birth.

Ecclesiastes 7:1 (KJV)

TRUST AND OBEY

Trust in the Lord with all your heart, and lean not on your own understanding; in all your ways acknowledge Him, and He shall direct your paths.

Proverbs 3:5–6 (NKJV)

Trust in the Lord, and do good; so you will dwell in the land, and enjoy security.

Psalm 37:3

Samuel replied: "Does the Lord delight in burnt offerings and sacrifices as much as in obeying the Lord? To obey is better than sacrifice, and to heed is better than the fat of rams."

1 Samuel 15:22 (NIV)

HONOR YOUR PARENTS

Honor your father and your mother, that your days may be long in the land which the Lord your God gives you.

Exodus 20:12

Children, obey your parents in the Lord, for this is right. "Honor your father and mother"—which is the first commandment with a promise—"so that it may go well with you and that you may enjoy long life on the earth."

Ephesians 6:1–3 (NIV)

Listen, my son, to your father's instruction and do not forsake your mother's teaching. They are a garland to grace your head and a chain to adorn your neck.

Proverbs 1:8–9 (NIV)

SEEK MULTIPLE WITNESSES

If he will not hear, take with you one or two more, that "by the mouth of two or three witnesses every word may be established."

Matthew 18:16 (NKJV)

No one is to be put to death on the testimony of only one witness.

Deuteronomy 17:6 (NIV)

This is the third time I am coming to you. In the mouth of two or three witnesses shall every word be established.

2 Corinthians 13:1 (KJV)

I have fought the good fight, I have finished the race, I have kept the faith.

2 Timothy 4:7

The Lord has dealt with me according to my righteousness; according to the cleanness of my hands he has rewarded me. For I have kept the ways of the Lord; I am not guilty of turning from my God.

2 Samuel 22:21–22 (NIV)

My son, give attention to my words; incline your ear to my sayings. Do not let them depart from your eyes; keep them in the midst of your heart; for they are life to those who find them, and health to all their flesh. Keep your heart with all diligence, for out of it spring the issues of life.

Proverbs 4:20–23 (NKJV)

PRAISE THE LORD

Praise the Lord! Praise God in his sanctuary; praise him in His mighty firmament! Praise him for his mighty deeds; praise him according to his exceeding greatness!

Psalm 150:1–2

I will declare your name to my people; in the assembly I will praise you.

Psalm 22:22 (NIV)

Praise be to the God and Father of our Lord Jesus Christ, the Father of compassion and the God of all comfort.

2 Corinthians 1:3 (NIV)

DO YOUR BEST

Whatever you do, do it all for the glory of God.

1 Corinthians 10:31 (NIV)

Let your light so shine before men, that they may see your good works, and glorify your Father which is in heaven.

Matthew 5:16 (KJV)

In this matter I give my advice: it is best for you now to complete what a year ago you began not only to do but to desire, so that your readiness in desiring it may be matched by your completing it out of what you have.

2 Corinthians 8:10–11

DON'T BE CHILDISH

When I was a child, I spoke like a child, I thought like a child, I reasoned like a child; when I became a man, I gave up childish ways.

1 Corinthians 13:11

Brothers and sisters, stop thinking like children. In regard to evil be infants, but in your thinking be adults.

1 Corinthians 14:20 (NIV)

I press toward the goal for the prize of the upward call of God in Christ Jesus. Therefore let us, as many as are mature, have this mind.

Philippians 3:14–15 (NKJV)

LOOK TO JESUS

[Look] unto Jesus, the author and finisher of our faith.

Hebrews 12:2 (NKJV)

You, beloved, building yourselves up on your most holy faith, praying in the Holy Spirit, keep yourselves in the love of God, looking for the mercy of our Lord Jesus Christ unto eternal life.

Jude 1:20–21 (NKJV)

Therefore, beloved, looking forward to these things, be diligent to be found by Him in peace, without spot and blameless.

2 Peter 3:14 (NKJV)

TELL THE TRUTH

An honest witness tells the truth, but a false witness tells lies. The words of the reckless pierce like swords, but the tongue of the wise brings healing. Truthful lips endure forever, but a lying tongue lasts only a moment.

Proverbs 12:17–19 (NIV)

You shall not bear false witness against your neighbor.

Exodus 20:16

Do not lie to one another, seeing that you have put off the old nature with its practices and have put on the new nature, which is being renewed in knowledge after the image of its creator.

Colossians 3:9–10

OBEY GOD'S COMMANDMENTS

See, I am setting before you today a blessing and a curse—the blessing if you obey the commands of the Lord your God that I am giving you today; the curse if you disobey the commands of the Lord your God and turn from the way that I command you today by following other gods, which you have not known.

Deuteronomy 11:26–28 (NIV)

You shall diligently keep the commandments of the Lord your God, and his testimonies, and his statutes, which he has commanded you. And you shall do what is right and good in the sight of the Lord.

Deuteronomy 6:17–18

Whoever has my commands and keeps them is the one who loves me. The one who loves me will be loved by my Father, and I too will love them and show myself to them.

John 14:21 (NIV)

FORGIVE AND FORGET

Peter came up and said to him, "Lord, how often shall my brother sin against me, and I forgive him? As many as seven times?" Jesus said to him, "I do not say to you seven times, but seventy times seven."

Matthew 18:21–22

Take heed to yourselves; if your brother sins, rebuke him, and if he repents, forgive him; and if he sins against you seven times in the day, and turns to you seven times, and says, "I repent," you must forgive him.

Luke 17:3–4

They all shall know me, from the least of them to the greatest, says the Lord; for I will forgive their iniquity, and I will remember their sin no more.

Jeremiah 31:34

DON'T LOOK BACK

Jesus said to him, "No one, who puts his hand to the plow and looks back is fit for the kingdom of God."

Luke 9:62

With the coming of dawn, the angels urged Lot, saying, "Hurry! Take your wife and your two daughters who are here, or you will be swept away when the city is punished." . . . As soon as [the angels] had brought them out, one of them said, "Flee for your lives! Don't look back, and don't stop anywhere in the plain! Flee to the mountains or you will be swept away!"

Genesis 19:15–17 (NIV)

Brothers and sisters, I do not consider myself yet to have taken hold of it. But one thing I do: Forgetting what is behind and straining toward what is ahead, I press on toward the goal to win the prize for which God has called me heavenward in Christ Jesus.

Philippians 3:13–14 (NIV)

CLAIM GOD'S PROMISES

We desire each one of you to show the same earnestness in realizing the full assurance of hope until the end, so that you may not be sluggish, but imitators of those who through faith and patience inherit the promises.

Hebrews 6:11–12

His divine power has granted to us all things that pertain to life and godliness, through the knowledge of him who called us to his own glory and excellence, by which he has granted to us his precious and very great promises, that through these you may escape from the corruption that is in the world because of passion, and become partakers of the divine nature.

2 Peter 1:3–4

No matter how many promises God has made, they are "Yes" in Christ. And so through him the "Amen" is spoken by us to the glory of God.

2 Corinthians 1:20 (NIV)

BE BORN AGAIN

Jesus replied, "Very truly I tell you, no one can see the kingdom of God unless they are born again."

John 3:3 (NIV)

You have been born again, not of perishable seed, but of imperishable, through the living and enduring word of God.

1 Peter 1:23 (NIV)

Yet to all who did receive him, to those who believed in his name, he gave the right to become children of God—children born not of natural descent, nor of human decision or a husband's will, but born of God.

John 1:12–13 (NIV)

GOD IS GOOD

Do not remember the sins of my youth, nor my transgressions; according to Your mercy remember me, for Your goodness' sake, O Lord. Good and upright is the Lord; therefore He teaches sinners in the way.

Psalm 25:7–8 (NKJV)

O give thanks to the Lord, for he is good; for his steadfast love endures for ever! Let the redeemed of the Lord say so, whom he has redeemed from trouble.

Psalm 107:1–2

[Jesus] said to him, "Why do you call Me good? No one is good but One, that is, God. But if you want to enter into life, keep the commandments."

Matthew 19:17 (NKJV)

HARD WORK PAYS

Whoever looks intently into the perfect law that gives freedom, and continues in it—not forgetting what they have heard, but doing it—they will be blessed in what they do.

James 1:25 (NIV)

You shall eat the fruit of the labor of your hands; you shall be happy, and it shall be well with you.

Psalm 128:2

Do you see a man skilful in his work? He will stand before kings; he will not stand before obscure men.

Proverbs 22:29

KEEP GOOD COMPANY

Do not be misled: "Bad company corrupts good character."

1 Corinthians 15:33 (NIV)

Now I have written to you not to keep company with anyone named a brother, who is sexually immoral, or covetous, or an idolater, or a reviler, or a drunkard, or an extortioner—not even to eat with such a person.

1 Corinthians 5:11 (NKJV)

In the name of the Lord Jesus Christ, we command you, brothers and sisters, to keep away from every believer who is idle and disruptive and does not live according to the teaching you received from us . . . Take special note of anyone who does not obey our instruction in this letter. Do not associate with them, in order that they may feel ashamed. Yet do not regard them as an enemy, but warn them as you would a fellow believer.

2 Thessalonians 3:6, 14–15 (NIV)

RESPECT YOUR ELDERS

Besides this, we have had earthly fathers to discipline us and we respected them. Shall we not much more be subject to the Father of spirits and live?

Hebrews 12:9

Stand up in the presence of the aged, show respect for the elderly and revere your God. I am the Lord.

Leviticus 19:32 (NIV)

Do not rebuke an older man but exhort him as you would a father.

1 Timothy 5:1

SPREAD THE WORD

Go therefore and make disciples of all nations, baptizing them in the name of the Father and of the Son and of the Holy Spirit, teaching them to observe all that I have commanded you.

Matthew 28:19–20

So the word of God spread. The number of disciples in Jerusalem increased rapidly, and a large number of priests became obedient to the faith.

Acts 6:7 (NIV)

The word of the Lord was being spread throughout all the region.

Acts 13:49 (NKJV)

WAIT UPON GOD

Wait on the Lord; be of good courage, and He shall strengthen your heart; Wait, I say, on the Lord!

Psalm 27:14 (NKJV)

He has made everything beautiful in its time. He has also set eternity in the human heart; yet no one can fathom what God has done from beginning to end.

Ecclesiastes 3:11 (NIV)

They that wait upon the Lord shall renew their strength; they shall mount up with wings as eagles; they shall run, and not be weary; and they shall walk, and not faint.

Isaiah 40:31 (KJV)

MAKE A PLAN

A man's heart plans his way, but the Lord directs his steps.

Proverbs 16:9 (NKJV)

The plans of the diligent lead to profit as surely as haste leads to poverty.

Proverbs 21:5 (NIV)

Commit your work to the Lord, and your plans will be established.

Proverbs 16:3

MONEY ISN'T EVERYTHING

No one can serve two masters. Either you will hate the one and love the other, or you will be devoted to the one and despise the other. You cannot serve both God and money.

Matthew 6:24 (NIV)

The love of money is a root of all kinds of evil. Some people, eager for money, have wandered from the faith and pierced themselves with many griefs.

1 Timothy 6:10 (NIV)

Command those who are rich in this present world not to be arrogant nor to put their hope in wealth, which is so uncertain, but to put their hope in God, who richly provides us with everything for our enjoyment.

1 Timothy 6:17 (NIV)

LEAD BY EXAMPLE

Join together in following my example, brothers and sisters, and just as you have us as a model, keep your eyes on those who live as we do.

Philippians 3:17 (NIV)

Now that I, your Lord and Teacher, have washed your feet, you also should wash one another's feet. I have set you an example that you should do as I have done for you.

John 13:14–15 (NIV)

Set the believers an example in speech and conduct, in love, in faith, in purity.

1 Timothy 4:12

JESUS IS LORD

I want you to understand that no one speaking by the Spirit of God ever says "Jesus be cursed!" and no one can say "Jesus is Lord" except by the Holy Spirit.

1 Corinthians 12:3

You know the message God sent to the people of Israel, announcing the good news of peace through Jesus Christ, who is Lord of all.

Acts 10:36 (NIV)

God has highly exalted him and bestowed on him the name which is above every name, that at the name of Jesus every knee should bow, in heaven and on earth and under the earth, and every tongue confess that Jesus Christ is Lord, to the glory of God the Father.

Philippians 2:9–11

HELP THE NEEDY

If any one has the world's goods and sees his brother in need, yet closes his heart against him, how does God's love abide in him?

1 John 3:17

He who oppresses a poor man insults his Maker, but he who is kind to the needy honors him.

Proverbs 14:31

There was not a needy person among them, for as many as were possessors of lands or houses sold them, and brought the proceeds of what was sold and laid it at the apostles' feet; and distribution was made to each as any had need.

Acts 4:34–35

LITTLE THINGS COUNT

His master said to him, "Well done, good and faithful servant; you have been faithful over a little, I will set you over much; enter into the joy of your master."

Matthew 25:23

Catch us the foxes, the little foxes, that spoil the vineyards, for our vineyards are in blossom.

Song of Solomon 2:15

[Jesus] said, "What shall we say the kingdom of God is like, or what parable shall we use to describe it? It is like a mustard seed, which is the smallest of all seeds on earth. Yet when planted, it grows and becomes the largest of all garden plants, with such big branches that the birds can perch in its shade."

Mark 4:30–32 (NIV)

RESIST THE DEVIL

Submit yourselves therefore to God. Resist the devil and he will flee from you.

James 4:7

Jesus said to him, "Away from me, Satan! For it is written: 'Worship the Lord your God, and serve him only.'"

Matthew 4:10 (NIV)

Jesus turned and said to Peter, "Get behind me, Satan! You are a stumbling block to me; you do not have in mind the concerns of God, but merely human concerns." Then Jesus said to his disciples, "Whoever wants to be my disciple must deny themselves and take up their cross and follow me."

Matthew 16:23–24 (NIV)

SILENCE IS GOLDEN

He who guards his mouth preserves his life; he who opens wide his lips comes to ruin.

Proverbs 13:3

If any one thinks he is religious, and does not bridle his tongue but deceives his heart, this man's religion is vain.

James 1:26

He who restrains his words has knowledge, and he who has a cool spirit is a man of understanding. Even a fool who keeps silent is considered wise; when he closes his lips, he is deemed intelligent.

Proverbs 17:27–28

USE KIND WORDS

Pleasant words are like a honeycomb, sweetness to the soul and health to the body.

Proverbs 16:24

Do not let any unwholesome talk come out of your mouths, but only what is helpful for building others up according to their needs, that it may benefit those who listen.

Ephesians 4:29 (NIV)

The thoughts of the wicked are an abomination to the Lord: but the words of the pure are pleasant words.

Proverbs 15:26 (KJV)

SHINE YOUR LIGHT

Let your light so shine before men, that they may see your good works, and glorify your Father which is in heaven.

Matthew 5:16 (KJV)

The righteous will shine like the sun in the kingdom of their Father.

Matthew 13:43

The path of the just is like the shining sun, that shines ever brighter unto the perfect day.

Proverbs 4:18 (NKJV)

NOTHING IS IMPOSSIBLE

With God nothing will be impossible.

Luke 1:37

Jesus looked at them and said to them, "With men this is impossible, but with God all things are possible."

Matthew 19:26

You have so little faith. Truly I tell you, if you have faith as small as a mustard seed, you can say to this mountain, "Move from here to there," and it will move. Nothing will be impossible for you.

Matthew 17:20 (NIV)

KNOWLEDGE IS POWER

My people are destroyed from lack of knowledge. "Because you have rejected knowledge, I also reject you as my priests; because you have ignored the law of your God, I also will ignore your children."

Hosea 4:6 (NIV)

My people are gone into captivity, because they have no knowledge: and their honourable men are famished, and their multitude dried up with thirst.

Isaiah 5:13 (KJV)

A wise man will hear, and will increase learning; and a man of understanding shall attain unto wise counsels: To understand a proverb, and the interpretation; the words of the wise, and their dark sayings. The fear of the Lord is the beginning of knowledge: but fools despise wisdom and instruction.

Proverbs 1:5–7 (KJV)

IN JESUS' NAME

If you ask anything in My name, I will do it.

John 14:14

Where two or three are gathered together in My name, I am there in the midst of them.

Matthew 18:20 (NKJV)

Whatever you do, in word or deed, do everything in the name of the Lord Jesus, giving thanks to God the Father through him.

Colossians 3:17

GIVE YOUR ALL

To the weak I became weak, that I might win the weak. I have become all things to all men, that I might by all means save some. I do it all for the sake of the gospel, that I may share in its blessings.

1 Corinthians 9:22–23

If anyone speaks, they should do so as one who speaks the very words of God. If anyone serves, they should do so with the strength God provides, so that in all things God may be praised through Jesus Christ. To him be the glory and the power for ever and ever. Amen.

1 Peter 4:11 (NIV)

Whatever you do, work at it with all your heart, as working for the Lord, not for human masters.

Colossians 3:23 (NIV)

DREAMS COME TRUE

A dream comes through much activity.

Ecclesiastes 5:3 (NKJV)

Take delight in the Lord, and he will give you the desires of your heart.

Psalm 37:4

O Lord God, You are God, and Your words are true, and You have promised this goodness to Your servant. Now therefore, let it please You to bless the house of Your servant, that it may continue before You forever; for You, O Lord God, have spoken it, and with Your blessing let the house of Your servant be blessed forever.

2 Samuel 7:28–29 (NKJV)

GOD WILL PROVIDE

My God shall supply all your need according to his riches in glory by Christ Jesus.

Philippians 4:19 (KJV)

I have been young, and now am old; yet I have not seen the righteous forsaken or his children begging bread.

Psalm 37:25

Abraham lifted up his eyes and looked, and behold, behind him was a ram, caught in a thicket by his horns; and Abraham went and took the ram, and offered it up as a burnt offering instead of his son. So Abraham called the name of that place The Lord will provide; as it is said to this day, "On the mount of the Lord it shall be provided."

Genesis 22:13–14

DO NOT GOSSIP

They learn to be idle, wandering about from house to house, and not only idle but also gossips and busybodies, saying things which they ought not.

1 Timothy 5:13 (NKJV)

Let no evil talk come out of your mouths, but only such as is good for edifying, as fits the occasion, that it may impart grace to those who hear.

Ephesians 4:29

A gossip betrays a confidence, but a trustworthy person keeps a secret.

Proverbs 11:13 (NIV)

BELIEVE IN MIRACLES

He who supplies the Spirit to you and works miracles among you, does He do it by the works of the law, or by the hearing of faith?—just as Abraham "believed God, and it was accounted to him for righteousness." Therefore know that only those who are of faith are sons of Abraham.

Galatians 3:5–7 (NKJV)

God did extraordinary miracles by the hands of Paul, so that handkerchiefs or aprons were carried away from his body to the sick, and diseases left them and the evil spirits came out of them.

Acts 19:11–12

To one is given through the Spirit the utterance of wisdom, and to another the utterance of knowledge according to the same Spirit, to another faith by the same Spirit, to another gifts of healing by the one Spirit, to another the working of miracles.

1 Corinthians 12:8–10

FINISH THE RACE

I have fought the good fight, I have finished the race, I have kept the faith.

2 Timothy 4:7

Since we are surrounded by so great a cloud of witnesses, let us also lay aside every weight, and sin which clings so closely, and let us run with perseverance the race that is set before us.

Hebrews 12:1

Do you not know that in a race all the runners compete, but only one receives the prize? So run that you may obtain it.

1 Corinthians 9:24

PRAYER CHANGES THINGS

The effective, fervent prayer of a righteous man avails much.

James 5:16 (NKJV)

Whatever you ask in my name, I will do it, that the Father may be glorified in the Son; if you ask anything in my name, I will do it.

John 14:13–14

Whatever you ask for in prayer, believe that you have received it, and it will be yours.

Mark 11:24 (NIV)

THINK YOU CAN

For as he thinks in his heart, so is he.

Proverbs 23:7 (NKJV)

Not that we are sufficient of ourselves to think any thing as of ourselves; but our sufficiency is of God.

2 Corinthians 3:5 (KJV)

I can do all things through Christ who strengthens me.

Philippians 4:13 (NKJV)

CRIME DOESN'T PAY

Although a wicked person who commits a hundred crimes may live a long time, I know that it will go better with those who fear God, who are reverent before him. Yet because the wicked do not fear God, it will not go well with them, and their days will not lengthen like a shadow.

Ecclesiastes 8:12–13 (NIV)

Let the thief no longer steal, but rather let him labor, doing honest work with his hands, so that he may be able to give to those in need.

Ephesians 4:28

The fear of the Lord prolongs days, but the years of the wicked will be shortened. The hope of the righteous will be gladness, but the expectation of the wicked will perish. The way of the Lord is strength for the upright, but destruction will come to the workers of iniquity.

Proverbs 10:27–29 (NKJV)

FAST AND PRAY

When you fast, do not look dismal, like the hypocrites, for they disfigure their faces that their fasting may be seen by men. Truly, I say to you, they have received their reward. But when you fast, anoint your head and wash your face, that your fasting may not be seen by men but by your Father who is in secret; and your Father who sees in secret will reward you.

Matthew 6:16–18

While they were worshiping the Lord and fasting, the Holy Spirit said, "Set apart for me Barnabas and Saul for the work to which I have called them." Then after fasting and praying they laid their hands on them and sent them off.

Acts 13:2–3

So we fasted and petitioned our God about this, and he answered our prayer.

Ezra 8:23 (NIV)

HASTE MAKES WASTE

The plans of the diligent lead to profit as surely as haste leads to poverty.

Proverbs 21:5 (NIV)

The end of a thing is better than its beginning; the patient in spirit is better than the proud in spirit. Do not hasten in your spirit to be angry, for anger rests in the bosom of fools.

Ecclesiastes 7:8–9 (NKJV)

He who is slow to anger has great understanding, but he who has a hasty temper exalts folly.

Proverbs 14:29

KEEP LOOKING UP

Keep yourselves in the love of God, looking for the mercy of our Lord Jesus Christ unto eternal life.

Jude 1:21 (KJV)

[The two men] said, "Men of Galilee, why do you stand looking into heaven? This Jesus, who was taken up from you into heaven, will come in the same way as you saw him go into heaven."

Acts 1:11

Denying ungodliness and worldly lusts, we should live soberly, righteously, and godly, in this present world; looking for that blessed hope, and the glorious appearing of the great God and our Saviour Jesus Christ.

Titus 2:12–13 (KJV)

LOVE YOUR NEIGHBOR

You shall not take vengeance or bear any grudge against the sons of your own people, but you shall love your neighbor as yourself: I am the Lord.

Leviticus 19:18

Your friend, and your father's friend, do not forsake; and do not go to your brother's house in the day of your calamity. Better is a neighbor who is near than a brother who is far away.

Proverbs 27:10

The commandments, "You shall not commit adultery, You shall not kill, You shall not steal, You shall not covet," and any other commandment, are summed up in this sentence, "You shall love your neighbor as yourself." Love does no wrong to a neighbor; therefore love is the fulfilling of the law.

Romans 13:9–10

READY, SET, GO

Sanctify the Lord God in your hearts, and always be ready to give a defense to everyone who asks you a reason for the hope that is in you, with meekness and fear.

1 Peter 3:15 (NKJV)

Moses finished speaking all these words to all Israel, and he said to them: "Set your hearts on all the words which I testify among you today, which you shall command your children to be careful to observe—all the words of this law.

Deuteronomy 32:45–46 (NKJV)

He said to them, "Go into all the world and preach the gospel to all creation."

Mark 16:15 (NIV)

STEADY DOES IT

We have become partakers of Christ if we hold the beginning of our confidence steadfast to the end.

Hebrews 3:14 (NKJV)

As for you, always be steady, endure suffering, do the work of an evangelist, fulfil your ministry.

2 Timothy 4:5

Continue in the faith, stable and steadfast, not shifting from the hope of the gospel which you heard, which has been preached to every creature under heaven, and of which I, Paul, became a minister.

Colossians 1:23

WALK BY FAITH

We walk by faith, not by sight.

2 Corinthians 5:7 (KJV)

Without faith it is impossible to please God, because anyone who comes to him must believe that he exists and that he rewards those who earnestly seek him.

Hebrews 11:6 (NIV)

As you therefore have received Christ Jesus the Lord, so walk in Him, rooted and built up in Him and established in the faith, as you have been taught, abounding in it with thanksgiving.

Colossians 2:6–7 (NKJV)

GIVE YOUR TITHE

"**B**ring the whole tithe into the storehouse, that there may be food in my house. Test me in this," says the Lord Almighty, "and see if I will not throw open the floodgates of heaven and pour out so much blessing that there will not be room enough to store it."

Malachi 3:10 (NIV)

You shall truly tithe all the increase of your grain that the field produces year by year.

Deuteronomy 14:22 (NKJV)

Honor the Lord with your wealth, with the firstfruits of all your crops; then your barns will be filled to overflowing, and your vats will brim over with new wine.

Proverbs 3:9–10 (NIV)

SAVE ME, JESUS

Believe in the Lord Jesus, and you will be saved, you and your household.

Acts 16:31

Neither is there salvation in any other: for there is none other name under heaven given among men, whereby we must be saved.

Acts 4:12 (KJV)

If you confess with your lips that Jesus is Lord and believe in your heart that God raised him from the dead, you will be saved. For man believes with his heart and so is justified, and he confesses with his lips and so is saved.

Romans 10:9–10

KEEP YOUR WORD

When a man vows a vow to the Lord, or swears an oath to bind himself by a pledge, he shall not break his word; he shall do according to all that proceeds out of his mouth.

Numbers 30:2

When you vow a vow to God, do not delay paying it; for he has no pleasure in fools. Pay what you vow. It is better that you should not vow than that you should vow and not pay.

Ecclesiastes 5:4–5

I have given my word to the Lord, and I cannot go back on it.

Judges 11:35 (NKJV)

LORD, HAVE MERCY

God, who is rich in mercy, out of the great love with which he loved us, even when we were dead through our trespasses, made us alive together with Christ (by grace you have been saved).

Ephesians 2:4–5

[God] says to Moses, "I will have mercy on whom I have mercy, and I will have compassion on whom I have compassion." So it depends not upon man's will or exertion, but upon God's mercy.

Romans 9:15–16

Oh, give thanks to the Lord, for He is good! For His mercy endures forever.

1 Chronicles 16:34 (NKJV)

DO NOT MURDER

You shall not murder.

Exodus 20:13 (NKJV)

You have heard that it was said to those of old, "You shall not murder, and whoever murders will be in danger of the judgment." But I say to you that whoever is angry with his brother without a cause shall be in danger of the judgment. And whoever says to his brother, "Raca!" shall be in danger of the council. But whoever says, "You fool!" shall be in danger of hell fire.

Matthew 5:21–22 (NKJV)

As for murderers . . . their lot shall be in the lake that burns with fire and sulphur, which is the second death.

Revelation 21:8

CONFESS YOUR SINS

If we confess our sins, he is faithful and just, and will forgive our sins and cleanse us from all unrighteousness. If we say we have not sinned, we make him a liar, and his word is not in us.

1 John 1:9–10

Confess your trespasses to one another, and pray for one another.

James 5:16 (NKJV)

Whoever conceals their sins does not prosper, but the one who confesses and renounces them finds mercy.

Proverbs 28:13 (NIV)

SHARE WITH OTHERS

Command them to do good, to be rich in good deeds, and to be generous and willing to share.

1 Timothy 6:18 (NIV)

Let him who is taught the word share all good things with him who teaches.

Galatians 6:6

Do not forget to do good and to share with others, for with such sacrifices God is pleased.

Hebrews 13:16 (NIV)

TIMING IS EVERYTHING

Daniel said: "Blessed be the name of God for ever and ever, to whom belong wisdom and might. He changes times and seasons; he removes kings and sets up kings; he gives wisdom to the wise."

Daniel 2:20–21

For everything there is a season, and a time for every matter under heaven: a time to be born, and a time to die; a time to plant, and a time to pluck up what is planted; a time to kill, and a time to heal; a time to break down, and a time to build up.

Ecclesiastes 3:1–3

He made known to us the mystery of his will according to his good pleasure, which he purposed in Christ, to be put into effect when the times reach their fulfillment—to bring unity to all things in heaven and on earth under Christ. In him we were also chosen.

Ephesians 1:9–11 (NIV)

MIND YOUR MANNERS

Make it your ambition to lead a quiet life: You should mind your own business and work with your hands, just as we told you, so that your daily life may win the respect of outsiders and so that you will not be dependent on anybody.

1 Thessalonians 4:11–12 (NIV)

Be not deceived: evil communications corrupt good manners.

1 Corinthians 15:33 (KJV)

As He which hath called you is holy, so be ye holy in all manner of conversation.

1 Peter 1:15 (KJV)

HOLD TO TRADITION

Brethren, stand firm and hold to the traditions which you were taught by us, either by word of mouth or by letter.

2 Thessalonians 2:15

My son, fear the Lord and the king; do not associate with those given to change.

Proverbs 24:21 (NKJV)

Remove not the ancient landmark which your fathers have set.

Proverbs 22:28

ABSTAIN FROM EVIL

Abstain from every form of evil.

1 Thessalonians 5:22

Dearly beloved, I beseech you as strangers and pilgrims, abstain from fleshly lusts, which war against the soul.

1 Peter 2:11 (KJV)

Evil shall slay the wicked, and those who hate the righteous shall be condemned. The Lord redeems the soul of His servants, and none of those who trust in Him shall be condemned.

Psalm 34:21–22 (NKJV)

DO WHAT'S RIGHT

Do what is right and good in the Lord's sight, so that it may go well with you and you may go in and take over the good land the Lord promised on oath to your ancestors.

Deuteronomy 6:18 (NIV)

"They do not know how to do right," says the Lord, "those who store up violence and robbery in their strongholds."

Amos 3:10

Every way of a man is right in his own eyes, but the Lord weighs the heart. To do righteousness and justice is more acceptable to the Lord than sacrifice.

Proverbs 21:2–3

I LOVE YOU

"I have loved you," says the Lord.

Malachi 1:2

For God so loved the world that he gave his only Son, that whoever believes in him should not perish but have eternal life.

John 3:16

This is my commandment, that you love one another as I have loved you.

John 15:12

TRUE LOVE WAITS

Let marriage be held in honor among all, and let the marriage bed be undefiled; for God will judge the immoral and adulterous.

Hebrews 13:4

Set your minds on things above, not on earthly things. For you died, and your life is now hidden with Christ in God. When Christ, who is your life, appears, then you also will appear with him in glory. Put to death, therefore, whatever belongs to your earthly nature: sexual immorality, impurity, lust, evil desires and greed, which is idolatry.

Colossians 3:2–5 (NIV)

It is God's will that you should be sanctified: that you should avoid sexual immorality; that each of you should learn to control your own body in a way that is holy and honorable, not in passionate lust like the pagans, who do not know God.

1 Thessalonians 4:3–5 (NIV)

DO NOT COVET

You shall not covet your neighbor's house. You shall not covet your neighbor's wife, or his male or female servant, his ox or donkey, or anything that belongs to your neighbor.

Exodus 20:17 (NIV)

[Jesus] said to them, "Take heed, and beware of all covetousness; for a man's life does not consist in the abundance of his possessions."

Luke 12:15

Let your conduct be without covetousness; be content with such things as you have. For He Himself has said, "I will never leave you nor forsake you."

Hebrews 13:5 (NKJV)

NEVER LOSE HOPE

Let us hold fast the confession of our hope without wavering, for he who promised is faithful.

Hebrews 10:23

For in this hope we were saved. Now hope that is seen is not hope. For who hopes for what he sees? But if we hope for what we do not see, we wait for it with patience.

Romans 8:24–25

There is surely a future hope for you, and your hope will not be cut off.

Proverbs 23:18 (NIV)

REMEMBER THE SABBATH

Remember the Sabbath day by keeping it holy. Six days you shall labor and do all your work, but the seventh day is a sabbath to the Lord your God. On it you shall not do any work . . . For in six days the Lord made the heavens and the earth, the sea, and all that is in them, but he rested on the seventh day. Therefore the Lord blessed the Sabbath day and made it holy.

Exodus 20:8–11 (NIV)

Say to the people of Israel, "You shall keep my sabbaths, for this is a sign between me and you throughout your generations, that you may know that I, the Lord, sanctify you."

Exodus 31:13

By the seventh day God had finished the work he had been doing; so on the seventh day he rested from all his work. Then God blessed the seventh day and made it holy, because on it he rested from all the work of creating that he had done.

Genesis 2:2–3 (NIV)

GOD BLESS YOU

The Lord bless you and keep you: The Lord make his face to shine upon you, and be gracious to you: The Lord lift up his countenance upon you, and give you peace.

Numbers 6:24–26

All these blessings shall come upon you and overtake you, if you obey the voice of the Lord your God. Blessed shall you be in the city, and blessed shall you be in the field. Blessed shall be the fruit of your body, and the fruit of your ground, and the fruit of your beasts, the increase of your cattle, and the young of your flock. Blessed shall be your basket and your kneading-trough. Blessed shall you be when you come in, and blessed shall you be when you go out.

Deuteronomy 28:2–6

Give generously to [the poor] and do so without a grudging heart; then because of this the Lord your God will bless you in all your work and in everything you put your hand to.

Deuteronomy 15:10 (NIV)

REMEMBER YOUR PAST

Then he remembered the days of old, of Moses his servant. Where is he who brought up out of the sea the shepherds of his flock? Where is he who put in the midst of them his holy Spirit?

Isaiah 63:11

You shall remember that you were a slave in the land of Egypt, and the Lord your God redeemed you; therefore I command you this today.

Deuteronomy 15:15

Remember how the Lord your God led you all the way in the wilderness these forty years, to humble and test you in order to know what was in your heart, whether or not you would keep his commands. He humbled you, causing you to hunger and then feeding you with manna . . . to teach you that man does not live on bread alone but on every word that comes from the mouth of the Lord.

Deuteronomy 8:2–3 (NIV)

BUSINESS BEFORE PLEASURE

[Jesus] said to them, "Why did you seek Me? Did you not know that I must be about My Father's business?"

Luke 2:49 (NKJV)

By faith Moses, when he was come to years, refused to be called the son of Pharaoh's daughter; choosing rather to suffer affliction with the people of God, than to enjoy the pleasures of sin for a season.

Hebrews 11:24–25 (KJV)

There will be terrible times in the last days. People will be lovers of themselves, lovers of money, boastful, proud, abusive, disobedient to their parents, ungrateful, unholy, without love, unforgiving, slanderous, without self-control, brutal, not lovers of the good, treacherous, rash, conceited, lovers of pleasure rather than lovers of God.

2 Timothy 3:1–4 (NIV)

DO NOT WORRY

Whenever you are arrested and brought to trial, do not worry beforehand about what to say. Just say whatever is given you at the time, for it is not you speaking, but the Holy Spirit.

Mark 13:11 (NIV)

Jesus said to his disciples: "Therefore I tell you, do not worry about your life, what you will eat; or about your body, what you will wear."

Luke 12:22 (NIV)

Do not worry about tomorrow, for tomorrow will worry about itself. Each day has enough trouble of its own.

Matthew 6:34 (NIV)

GET TO WORK

We are his workmanship, created in Christ Jesus for good works, which God prepared beforehand, that we should walk in them.

Ephesians 2:10

Verily, verily, I say unto you, He that believeth on me, the works that I do shall he do also; and greater works than these shall he do; because I go unto my Father.

John 14:12 (KJV)

What does it profit, my brethren, if a man says he has faith but has not works? Can his faith save him? . . . So faith by itself, if it has no works, is dead.

James 2:14, 17

JUST SAY NO

For the grace of God has appeared that offers salvation to all people. It teaches us to say "No" to ungodliness and worldly passions, and to live self-controlled, upright and godly lives in this present age.

Titus 2:11–12 (NIV)

Do not enter the path of the wicked, and do not walk in the way of evil men. Avoid it; do not go on it; turn away from it and pass on.

Proverbs 4:14–15

But you, O man of God, flee these things and pursue righteousness, godliness, faith, love, patience, gentleness.

1 Timothy 6:11 (NKJV)

GOD ANSWERS PRAYER

Call to me and I will answer you, and will tell you great and hidden things which you have not known.

Jeremiah 33:3

He will call on me, and I will answer him; I will be with him in trouble, I will deliver him and honor him. With long life I will satisfy him and show him my salvation.

Psalm 91:15–16 (NIV)

[The Lord] shall regard the prayer of the destitute, and shall not despise their prayer.

Psalm 102:17 (NKJV)

Assemble the people, men, women, and little ones, and the sojourner within your towns, that they may hear and learn to fear the Lord your God, and be careful to do all the words of this law, and that their children, who have not known it, may hear and learn to fear the Lord your God, as long as you live in the land which you are going over the Jordan to possess.

Deuteronomy 31:12–13

Take my yoke upon you, and learn from me; for I am gentle and lowly in heart, and you will find rest for your souls.

Matthew 11:29

A wise man will hear and increase learning, and a man of understanding will attain wise counsel.

Proverbs 1:5 (NKJV)

PEACE, BE STILL

Be still, and know that I am God; I am exalted among the nations, I am exalted in the earth!

Psalm 46:10

Be still before the Lord, and wait patiently for him; fret not yourself over him who prospers in his way, over the man who carries out evil devices!

Psalm 37:7

[Jesus] awoke and rebuked the wind, and said to the sea, "Peace! Be still!" And the wind ceased, and there was a great calm.

Mark 4:39

STOP, LOOK, LISTEN

Stop and consider the wondrous works of God.

Job 37:14

As for me, I will look to the Lord, I will wait for the God of my salvation; my God will hear me.

Micah 7:7

Listen to advice and accept instruction, that you may gain wisdom for the future.

Proverbs 19:20

DON'T GET DRUNK

Do not get drunk on wine, which leads to debauchery. Instead, be filled with the Spirit.

Ephesians 5:18 (NIV)

You are all sons of light and sons of the day. We are not of the night nor of darkness. Therefore let us not sleep, as others do, but let us watch and be sober. For those who sleep, sleep at night, and those who get drunk are drunk at night. But let us who are of the day be sober.

1 Thessalonians 5:5–8 (NKJV)

Let us behave decently, as in the daytime, not in carousing and drunkenness, not in sexual immorality and debauchery, not in dissension and jealousy. Rather, clothe yourselves with the Lord Jesus Christ, and do not think about how to gratify the desires of the flesh.

Romans 13:13–14 (NIV)

ASK FOR WISDOM

If any of you lacks wisdom, let him ask God, who gives to all men generously and without reproaching, and it will be given him.

James 1:5

"Give to Your servant an understanding heart to judge Your people, that I may discern between good and evil. For who is able to judge this great people of Yours?" The speech pleased the Lord, that Solomon had asked this thing.

1 Kings 3:9–10 (NKJV)

The wisdom that is from above is first pure, then peaceable, gentle, and easy to be intreated, full of mercy and good fruits, without partiality, and without hypocrisy.

James 3:17 (KJV)

CHOOSE THIS DAY

If you be unwilling to serve the Lord, choose this day whom you will serve, whether the gods your fathers served in the region beyond the River, or the gods of the Amorites in whose land you dwell; but as for me and my house, we will serve the Lord.

Joshua 24:15

Elijah went before the people and said, "How long will you waver between two opinions? If the Lord is God, follow him; but if Baal is God, follow him." But the people said nothing.

1 Kings 18:21 (NIV)

If you obey the voice of the Lord your God, being careful to do all his commandments which I command you this day, the Lord your God will set you high above all the nations of the earth. And all these blessings shall come upon you and overtake you, if you obey the voice of the Lord your God.

Deuteronomy 28:1–2

IT TAKES TEAMWORK

For as in one body we have many members, and all the members do not have the same function, so we, though many, are one body in Christ, and individually members one of another. Having gifts that differ according to the grace given to us, let us use them.

Romans 12:4–6

There are diversities of gifts, but the same Spirit. There are differences of ministries, but the same Lord. And there are diversities of activities, but it is the same God who works all in all. But the manifestation of the Spirit is given to each one for the profit of all.

1 Corinthians 12:4–7 (NKJV)

Lead a life worthy of the calling to which you have been called, with all lowliness and meekness, with patience, forbearing one another in love, eager to maintain the unity of the Spirit in the bond of peace.

Ephesians 4:1–3

SAY THE WORD

Keep this Book of the Law always on your lips; meditate on it day and night, so that you may be careful to do everything written in it. Then you will be prosperous and successful.

Joshua 1:8 (NIV)

If you abide in me, and my words abide in you, ask whatever you will, and it shall be done for you.

John 15:7

Truly, I say to you, whoever says to this mountain, "Be taken up and cast into the sea," and does not doubt in his heart, but believes that what he says will come to pass, it will be done for him.

Mark 11:23

WORSHIP THE LORD

Because He is your Lord, worship Him.

Psalm 45:11 (NKJV)

Oh come, let us worship and bow down, let us kneel before the Lord, our Maker.

Psalm 95:6 (NKJV)

I saw another angel fly in the midst of heaven, having the everlasting gospel to preach unto them that dwell on the earth, and to every nation, and kindred, and tongue, and people, saying with a loud voice, Fear God, and give glory to him; for the hour of his judgment is come: and worship him that made heaven, and earth, and the sea, and the fountains of waters.

Revelation 14:6–7 (KJV)

DISCIPLINE YOUR BODY

I discipline my body and bring it into subjection, lest, when I have preached to others, I myself should become disqualified.

1 Corinthians 9:27 (NKJV)

While bodily training is of some value, godliness is of value in every way, as it holds promise for the present life and also for the life to come.

1 Timothy 4:8

You were bought at a price; therefore glorify God in your body and in your spirit, which are God's.

1 Corinthians 6:20 (NKJV)

ANYTHING IS POSSIBLE

The Lord said to Abraham, "Why did Sarah laugh and say, 'Will I really have a child, now that I am old?' Is anything too hard for the Lord?"

Genesis 18:13–14 (NIV)

If you ask anything in my name, I will do it.

John 14:14

Jesus looked at them and said to them, "With men this is impossible, but with God all things are possible."

Matthew 19:26

FAITH, HOPE, LOVE

Faith is the substance of things hoped for, the evidence of things not seen.

Hebrews 11:1 (KJV)

Guide me in your truth and teach me, for you are God my Savior, and my hope is in you all day long.

Psalm 25:5 (NIV)

And now these three remain: faith, hope and love. But the greatest of these is love.

1 Corinthians 13:13 (NIV)

I AM GOD

Moses said to God, "Suppose I go to the Israelites and say to them, 'The God of your fathers has sent me to you,' and they ask me, 'What is his name?' Then what shall I tell them?" God said to Moses, "I am who I am. This is what you are to say to the Israelites: 'I am has sent me to you.'"

Exodus 3:13–14 (NIV)

I am the Lord your God, who brought you out of the land of Egypt.

Psalm 81:10 (NKJV)

Be still, and know that I am God. I am exalted among the nations, I am exalted in the earth!

Psalm 46:10

DON'T BE FOOLISH

The fear of the Lord is the beginning of knowledge: but fools despise wisdom and instruction.

Proverbs 1:7 (KJV)

The wisdom of the prudent is to understand his way, but the folly of fools is deceit. Fools mock at sin, but among the upright there is favor.

Proverbs 14:8–9 (NKJV)

The fool says in his heart, "There is no God." They are corrupt, they do abominable deeds, there is none that does good.

Psalm 14:1

THANK THE LORD

Giving thanks always for all things unto God and the Father in the name of our Lord Jesus Christ.

Ephesians 5:20 (KJV)

In every thing give thanks: for this is the will of God in Christ Jesus concerning you.

1 Thessalonians 5:18 (KJV)

Let them thank the Lord for his steadfast love, for his wonderful works to the sons of men!

Psalm 107:8

NEVER STOP LEARNING

Whatever things were written before were written for our learning, that we through the patience and comfort of the Scriptures might have hope.

Romans 15:4 (NKJV)

Assemble the people, men, women, and little ones, and the sojourner within your towns, that they may hear and learn to fear the Lord your God, and be careful to do all the words of this law, and that their children, who have not known it, may hear and learn to fear the Lord your God, as long as you live in the land which you are going over the Jordan to possess.

Deuteronomy 31:12–13

A wise man will hear and increase learning, and a man of understanding will attain wise counsel.

Proverbs 1:5 (NKJV)

I CAN'T COMPLAIN

Do all things without complaining and disputing, that you may become blameless and harmless, children of God without fault in the midst of a crooked and perverse generation, among whom you shine as lights in the world.

Philippians 2:14–15 (NKJV)

Do not become idolaters as were some of them . . . nor complain, as some of them also complained, and were destroyed by the destroyer.

1 Corinthians 10:7, 10 (NKJV)

The people complained about their hardships in the hearing of the Lord, and when he heard them his anger was aroused.

Numbers 11:1 (NIV)

YOUR KINGDOM COME

Your kingdom come. Your will be done on earth as it is in heaven.

Matthew 6:10 (NKJV)

Jesus began to preach, saying, "Repent, for the kingdom of heaven is at hand."

Matthew 4:17

The Spirit and the Bride say, "Come." And let him who hears say, "Come." And let him who is thirsty come, let him who desires take the water of life without price . . . He who testifies to these things says, "Surely I am coming soon." Amen. Come, Lord Jesus!

Revelation 22:17, 20

DON'T SOW SPARINGLY

Remember this: Whoever sows sparingly will also reap sparingly, and whoever sows generously will also reap generously.

2 Corinthians 9:6 (NIV)

Do not be deceived; God is not mocked, for whatever a man sows, that he will also reap . . . And let us not grow weary in well-doing, for in due season we shall reap, if we do not lose heart.

Galatians 6:7, 9

Give, and it will be given to you; good measure, pressed down, shaken together, running over, will be put into your lap. For the measure you give will be the measure you get back.

Luke 6:38

GOD'S IN CONTROL

In [Christ] also we have obtained an inheritance, being predestined according to the purpose of Him who works all things according to the counsel of His will.

Ephesians 1:11 (NKJV)

Are not two sparrows sold for a penny? And not one of them will fall to the ground without your Father's will.

Matthew 10:29

Remember the former things of old; for I am God, and there is no other; I am God, and there is none like me, declaring the end from the beginning and from ancient times things not yet done, saying, "My counsel shall stand, and I will accomplish all my purpose."

Isaiah 46:9–10

BE THEREFORE HOLY

As he which hath called you is holy, so be ye holy in all manner of conversation; because it is written, be ye holy; for I am holy.

1 Peter 1:15–16 (KJV)

He chose us in him before the foundation of the world, that we should be holy and blameless before him.

Ephesians 1:4

Having therefore these promises, dearly beloved, let us cleanse ourselves from all filthiness of the flesh and spirit, perfecting holiness in the fear of God.

2 Corinthians 7:1 (KJV)

DUTY, HONOR, COUNTRY

Does [the master] thank the servant because he did what was commanded? So you also, when you have done all that is commanded you, say, "We are unworthy servants; we have only done what was our duty."

Luke 17:9–10

Having your conduct honorable among the Gentiles, that when they speak against you as evildoers, they may, by your good works which they observe, glorify God in the day of visitation . . . Honor all people. Love the brotherhood. Fear God. Honor the king.

1 Peter 2:12, 17 (NKJV)

People who speak thus make it clear that they are seeking a homeland . . . They desire a better country, that is, a heavenly one. Therefore God is not ashamed to be called their God, for he has prepared for them a city.

Hebrews 11:14, 16

IN CHRIST ALONE

For by grace you have been saved through faith; and this is not your own doing, it is the gift of God—not because of works, lest any man should boast.

Ephesians 2:8–9

Do not be ashamed of the testimony about our Lord or of me his prisoner. Rather, join with me in suffering for the gospel, by the power of God. He has saved us and called us to a holy life—not because of anything we have done but because of his own purpose and grace. This grace was given us in Christ Jesus before the beginning of time.

2 Timothy 1:8–9 (NIV)

I have been crucified with Christ; it is no longer I who live, but Christ lives in me; and the life which I now live in the flesh I live by faith in the Son of God, who loved me and gave Himself for me. I do not set aside the grace of God; for if righteousness comes through the law, then Christ died in vain.

Galatians 2:20–21 (NKJV)

COMFORT ONE ANOTHER

Praise be to the God and Father of our Lord Jesus Christ, the Father of compassion and the God of all comfort, who comforts us in all our troubles, so that we can comfort those in any trouble with the comfort we ourselves receive from God.

2 Corinthians 1:3–4 (NIV)

As one whom his mother comforts, so I will comfort you; you shall be comforted in Jerusalem.

Isaiah 66:13

Comfort each other and edify one another, just as you also are doing.

1 Thessalonians 5:11 (NKJV)

PRIDE BRINGS DESTRUCTION

Pride goes before destruction, and a haughty spirit before a fall.

Proverbs 16:18

Do not love the world or the things in the world. If any one loves the world, love for the Father is not in him. For all that is in the world, the lust of the flesh and the lust of the eyes and the pride of life, is not of the Father but is of the world.

1 John 2:15–16

A man's pride shall bring him low: but honour shall uphold the humble in spirit.

Proverbs 29:23 (KJV)

TAKE A STAND

Therefore, my brothers and sisters, you whom I love and long for, my joy and crown, stand firm in the Lord in this way, dear friends!

Philippians 4:1 (NIV)

Take the whole armor of God, that you may be able to withstand in the evil day, and having done all, to stand. Stand therefore, having girded your loins with truth, and having put on the breastplate of righteousness.

Ephesians 6:13–14

Let any one who thinks that he stands take heed lest he fall.

1 Corinthians 10:12

LISTEN TO GOD

Why spend money on what is not bread, and your labor on what does not satisfy? Listen, listen to me, and eat what is good, and you will delight in the richest of fare.

Isaiah 55:2 (NIV)

Wisdom calls aloud outside; she raises her voice in the open squares. She cries out in the chief concourses, at the openings of the gates in the city she speaks her words: . . . Turn at my rebuke; surely I will pour out my spirit on you; I will make my words known to you.

Proverbs 1:20–21, 23 (NKJV)

The Lord passed by, and a great and strong wind rent the mountains . . . And after the earthquake a fire, but the Lord was not in the fire; and after the fire a still small voice. And when Elijah heard it, he . . . went out and stood at the entrance of the cave. And behold, there came a voice to him, and said, "What are you doing here, Elijah?"

1 Kings 19:11–13

SERVE THE LORD

Serve the Lord with gladness! Come into his presence with singing! Know that the Lord is God! It is he that made us, and we are his; we are his people, and the sheep of his pasture.

Psalm 100:2–3

Whoever wants to become great among you must be your servant, and whoever wants to be first must be your slave— just as the Son of Man did not come to be served, but to serve, and to give his life as a ransom for many.

Matthew 20:26–28 (NIV)

Whatever you do, do it heartily, as to the Lord and not to men, knowing that from the Lord you will receive the reward of the inheritance; for you serve the Lord Christ.

Colossians 3:23–24 (NKJV)

NEVER GIVE UP

Do not throw away your confidence, which has a great reward. For you have need of endurance, so that you may do the will of God and receive what is promised.

Hebrews 10:35–36

Let us not become weary in doing good, for at the proper time we will reap a harvest if we do not give up.

Galatians 6:9 (NIV)

We are made partakers of Christ, if we hold the beginning of our confidence stedfast unto the end.

Hebrews 3:14 (KJV)

SHOW AND TELL

Someone will say, "You have faith, and I have works." Show me your faith without your works, and I will show you my faith by my works.

James 2:18 (NKJV)

O Lord, open my lips, and my mouth shall show forth Your praise.

Psalm 51:15 (NKJV)

Jesus . . . said, "Go home to your own people and tell them how much the Lord has done for you, and how he has had mercy on you."

Mark 5:19 (NIV)

LAY THE FOUNDATION

As for everyone who comes to me and hears my words and puts them into practice, I will show you what they are like. They are like a man building a house, who dug down deep and laid the foundation on rock. When a flood came, the torrent struck that house but could not shake it, because it was well built.

Luke 6:47–48 (NIV)

As the whirlwind passeth, so is the wicked no more: but the righteous is an everlasting foundation . . . The way of the Lord is strength to the upright.

Proverbs 10:25, 29 (KJV)

According to the grace of God given to me, like a skilled master builder I laid a foundation, and another man is building upon it. Let each man take care how he builds upon it. For no other foundation can any one lay than that which is laid, which is Jesus Christ.

1 Corinthians 3:10–11

SEARCH THE SCRIPTURES

Search from the book of the Lord, and read: not one of these shall fail.

Isaiah 34:16 (NKJV)

All scripture is given by inspiration of God, and is profitable for doctrine, for reproof, for correction, for instruction in righteousness: That the man of God may be perfect, thoroughly furnished unto all good works.

2 Timothy 3:16–17 (KJV)

This book of the law shall not depart out of your mouth, but you shall meditate on it day and night, that you may be careful to do according to all that is written in it; for then you shall make your way prosperous, and then you shall have good success.

Joshua 1:8

GO TO CHURCH

I was glad when they said to me, "Let us go to the house of the Lord!"

Psalm 122:1

Let us consider one another in order to stir up love and good works, not forsaking the assembling of ourselves together, as is the manner of some, but exhorting one another, and so much the more as you see the Day approaching.

Hebrews 10:24–25 (NKJV)

They worshipped Him, and returned to Jerusalem with great joy: and were continually in the temple, praising and blessing God. Amen.

Luke 24:52–53 (KJV)

JUST BE YOURSELF

There are diversities of gifts, but the same Spirit. There are differences of ministries, but the same Lord. And there are diversities of activities, but it is the same God who works all in all.

1 Corinthians 12:4–6 (NKJV)

Let each one remain in the same calling in which he was called . . . Brethren, let each one remain with God in that state in which he was called.

1 Corinthians 7:20, 24 (NKJV)

Do not answer a fool according to his folly, or you yourself will be just like him.

Proverbs 26:4 (NIV)

HAVE SOME PATIENCE

My brethren, count it all joy when you fall into various trials, knowing that the testing of your faith produces patience. But let patience have its perfect work, that you may be perfect and complete, lacking nothing.

James 1:2–4 (NKJV)

By your patience possess your souls.

Luke 21:19 (NKJV)

Be patient, therefore, brethren, until the coming of the Lord. Behold, the farmer waits for the precious fruit of the earth, being patient over it until it receives the early and the late rain. You also be patient. Establish your hearts, for the coming of the Lord is at hand.

James 5:7–8

FLEE FROM ADULTERY

You shall not commit adultery.

Exodus 20:14 (NIV)

Flee from sexual immorality. All other sins a person commits are outside the body, but whoever sins sexually, sins against their own body.

1 Corinthians 6:18 (NIV)

A man who commits adultery has no sense; whoever does so destroys himself.

Proverbs 6:32 (NIV)

KEEP IT SIMPLE

Our boasting is this: the testimony of our conscience that we conducted ourselves in the world in simplicity and godly sincerity, not with fleshly wisdom but by the grace of God, and more abundantly toward you.

2 Corinthians 1:12 (NKJV)

Continuing daily with one accord in the temple, and breaking bread from house to house, they ate their food with gladness and simplicity of heart, praising God and having favor with all the people. And the Lord added to the church daily those who were being saved.

Acts 2:46–47 (NKJV)

I fear, lest somehow, as the serpent deceived Eve by his craftiness, so your minds may be corrupted from the simplicity that is in Christ.

2 Corinthians 11:3 (NKJV)

SING TO GOD

Sing to God, sing in praise of his name, extol him who rides on the clouds; rejoice before him—his name is the Lord.

Psalm 68:4 (NIV)

Sing praises to the Lord, O you his saints, and give thanks to his holy name.

Psalm 30:4

Sing to God, O kingdoms of the earth; sing praises to the Lord.

Psalm 68:32

REST IN HIM

Rest in the Lord, and wait patiently for Him; do not fret because of him who prospers in his way, because of the man who brings wicked schemes to pass.

Psalm 37:7 (NKJV)

There remains a sabbath rest for the people of God; for whoever enters God's rest also ceases from his labors as God did from his. Let us therefore strive to enter that rest.

Hebrews 4:9–11

Come to me, all who labor and are heavy laden, and I will give you rest. Take my yoke upon you, and learn from me; for I am gentle and lowly in heart, and you will find rest for your souls. For my yoke is easy, and my burden is light.

Matthew 11:28–30

TRY, TRY AGAIN

Let us not become weary in doing good, for at the proper time we will reap a harvest if we do not give up.

Galatians 6:9 (NIV)

As for you, continue in what you have learned and have firmly believed, knowing from whom you learned it.

2 Timothy 3:14

Do not throw away your confidence, which has a great reward. For you have need of endurance, so that you may do the will of God and receive what is promised.

Hebrews 10:35–36

YOU ARE COMMISSIONED

He said to them, "Go into all the world and preach the gospel to all creation. Whoever believes and is baptized will be saved, but whoever does not believe will be condemned."

Mark 16:15–16 (NIV)

You shall receive power when the Holy Spirit has come upon you; and you shall be my witnesses in Jerusalem and in all Judea and Samaria and to the end of the earth.

Acts 1:8

Go therefore and make disciples of all nations, baptizing them in the name of the Father and of the Son and of the Holy Spirit, teaching them to observe all that I have commanded you.

Matthew 28:19–20

LOVE CONQUERS ALL

Beloved, let us love one another; for love is of God, and he who loves is born of God and knows God. He who does not love does not know God; for God is love.

1 John 4:7–8

So faith, hope, love abide, these three; but the greatest of these is love.

1 Corinthians 13:13

I saw when the Lamb opened one of the seals, and I heard, as it were the noise of thunder, one of the four beasts saying, Come and see. And I saw, and behold a white horse: and he that sat on him had a bow; and a crown was given unto him: and he went forth conquering, and to conquer.

Revelation 6:1–2 (KJV)

KNOW GOD'S WORD

I have hidden your word in my heart that I might not sin against you.

Psalm 119:11 (NIV)

Jesus answered, "It is written: 'Man shall not live on bread alone, but on every word that comes from the mouth of God.'"

Matthew 4:4 (NIV)

Neither have I gone back from the commandment of his lips; I have esteemed the words of his mouth more than my necessary food.

Job 23:12 (KJV)

SIN NO MORE

When Jesus had raised Himself up and saw no one but the woman, He said to her, "Woman, where are those accusers of yours? Has no one condemned you?" She said, "No one, Lord." And Jesus said to her, "Neither do I condemn you; go and sin no more."

John 8:10–11 (NKJV)

Do not be like your ancestors, to whom the earlier prophets proclaimed: This is what the Lord Almighty says: "Turn from your evil ways and your evil practices." But they would not listen or pay attention to me, declares the Lord.

Zechariah 1:4 (NIV)

Afterward, Jesus found him in the temple, and said to him, "See, you are well! Sin no more, that nothing worse befall you."

John 5:14

NOW'S THE TIME

[God] says, "At the acceptable time I have listened to you, and helped you on the day of salvation." Behold, now is the acceptable time; behold, now is the day of salvation.

2 Corinthians 6:2

Blessed is he who reads aloud the words of the prophecy, and blessed are those who hear, and who keep what is written therein; for the time is near.

Revelation 1:3

Last year you were the first not only to give but also to have the desire to do so. Now finish the work, so that your eager willingness to do it may be matched by your completion of it, according to your means.

2 Corinthians 8:10–11 (NIV)

COUNT IT JOY

My brethren, count it all joy when you fall into various trials, knowing that the testing of your faith produces patience. But let patience have its perfect work, that you may be perfect and complete, lacking nothing.

James 1:2–4 (NKJV)

They departed from the presence of the council, rejoicing that they were counted worthy to suffer shame for his name.

Acts 5:41 (KJV)

More than that, we rejoice in our sufferings, knowing that suffering produces endurance, and endurance produces character, and character produces hope.

Romans 5:3–4

ALL FOR ONE

Christ's love compels us, because we are convinced that one died for all, and therefore all died. And he died for all, that those who live should no longer live for themselves but for him who died for them and was raised again.

2 Corinthians 5:14–15 (NIV)

I pray for them. I am not praying for the world, but for those you have given me, for they are yours . . . Holy Father, protect them by the power of your name, the name you gave me, so that they may be one as we are one.

John 17:9, 11 (NIV)

Be completely humble and gentle; be patient, bearing with one another in love. Make every effort to keep the unity of the Spirit through the bond of peace. There is one body and one Spirit, just as you were called to one hope when you were called; one Lord, one faith, one baptism; one God and Father of all, who is over all and through all and in all.

Ephesians 4:2–6 (NIV)

JESUS IS KING

Over his head they put the charge against him, which read, "This is Jesus the King of the Jews."

Matthew 27:37

I charge you to keep the commandment unstained and free from reproach until the appearing of our Lord Jesus Christ; and this will be made manifest at the proper time by the blessed and only Sovereign, the King of kings and Lord of lords, who alone has immortality and dwells in unapproachable light, whom no man has ever seen or can see. To him be honor and eternal dominion. Amen.

1 Timothy 6:14-16

They will make war on the Lamb, and the Lamb will conquer them, for he is Lord of lords and King of kings, and those with him are called and chosen and faithful.

Revelation 17:14

TAKE IT SLOW

He who is slow to anger has great understanding, but he who has a hasty temper exalts folly.

Proverbs 14:29

Know this, my beloved brethren. Let every man be quick to hear, slow to speak, slow to anger, for the anger of man does not work the righteousness of God.

James 1:19–20

He who is slow to anger is better than the mighty, and he who rules his spirit than he who takes a city.

Proverbs 16:32

ACTIONS SPEAK LOUDLY

What does it profit, my brethren, if a man says he has faith but has not works? Can his faith save him? If a brother or sister is ill-clad and in lack of daily food, and one of you says to them, "Go in peace, be warmed and filled," without giving them the things needed for the body, what does it profit? So faith by itself, if it has no works, is dead.

James 2:14–17

When you give to the needy, do not announce it with trumpets, as the hypocrites do in the synagogues and on the streets, to be honored by others. Truly I tell you, they have received their reward in full.

Matthew 6:2 (NIV)

He who looks into the perfect law, the law of liberty, and perseveres, being no hearer that forgets but a doer that acts, he shall be blessed in his doing.

James 1:25

LOVE THE LORD

Love the Lord your God with all your heart and with all your soul and with all your strength.

Deuteronomy 6:5 (NIV)

And now, Israel, what does the Lord your God require of you, but to fear the Lord your God, to walk in all his ways, to love him, to serve the Lord your God with all your heart and with all your soul.

Deuteronomy 10:12

[Jesus] said to him, "You shall love the Lord your God with all your heart, and with all your soul, and with all your mind. This is the great and first commandment. And a second is like it, You shall love your neighbor as yourself. On these two commandments depend all the law and the prophets."

Matthew 22:37–40

DO NOT LIE

Do not lie to one another, seeing that you have put off the old nature with its practices.

Colossians 3:9

As for . . . all liars, their lot shall be in the lake that burns with fire and sulphur, which is the second death.

Revelation 21:8

Blessed are those who do His commandments, that they may have the right to the tree of life, and may enter through the gates into the city. But outside are dogs and sorcerers and sexually immoral and murderers and idolaters, and whoever loves and practices a lie.

Revelation 22:14–15 (NKJV)

APPEARANCES CAN DECEIVE

Do not judge by appearances, but judge with right judgment.

John 7:24

Beware of false prophets, who come to you in sheep's clothing but inwardly are ravenous wolves.

Matthew 7:15

The Lord said to Samuel, "Do not consider his appearance or his height, for I have rejected him. The Lord does not look at the things people look at. People look at the outward appearance, but the Lord looks at the heart."

1 Samuel 16:7 (NIV)

MAINTAIN YOUR SELF-CONTROL

Make every effort to add to your faith goodness; and to goodness, knowledge; and to knowledge, self-control; and to self-control, perseverance; and to perseverance, godliness.

2 Peter 1:5–6 (NIV)

The fruit of the Spirit is love, joy, peace, patience, kindness, goodness, faithfulness, gentleness, self-control; against such there is no law.

Galatians 5:22–23

Better a patient person than a warrior, one with self-control than one who takes a city.

Proverbs 16:32 (NIV)

LIVE BY FAITH

Still the vision awaits its time; it hastens to the end—it will not lie. If it seem slow, wait for it; it will surely come, it will not delay. Behold, he whose soul is not upright in him shall fail, but the righteous shall live by his faith.

Habakkuk 2:3–4

For we live by faith, not by sight.

2 Corinthians 5:7 (NIV)

For I am not ashamed of the gospel of Christ, for it is the power of God to salvation for everyone who believes, for the Jew first and also for the Greek. For in it the righteousness of God is revealed from faith to faith; as it is written, "The just shall live by faith."

Romans 1:16–17 (NKJV)

FOLLOW THE RULES

An athlete is not crowned unless he competes according to the rules.

2 Timothy 2:5

By this we know that we love the children of God, when we love God and obey his commandments.

1 John 5:2

The law of the Lord is perfect, reviving the soul; the testimony of the Lord is sure, making wise the simple; the precepts of the Lord are right, rejoicing the heart; the commandment of the Lord is pure, enlightening the eyes.

Psalm 19:7–8

JESUS IS SAVIOR

For to you is born this day in the city of David a Savior, who is Christ the Lord.

Luke 2:11

They said to the woman, "Now we believe, not because of what you said, for we ourselves have heard Him and we know that this is indeed the Christ, the Savior of the world."

John 4:42 (NKJV)

Do not be ashamed then of testifying to our Lord, nor of me his prisoner, but share in suffering for the gospel in the power of God, who saved us and called us with a holy calling, not in virtue of our works but in virtue of his own purpose and the grace which he gave us in Christ Jesus ages ago, and now has manifested through the appearing of our Savior Christ Jesus, who abolished death and brought life and immortality to light through the gospel.

2 Timothy 1:8–10

BE SPIRIT FILLED

Be filled with the Spirit.

For this reason I bow my knees before the Father . . . that according to the riches of his glory he may grant you to be strengthened with might through his Spirit in the inner man, and that Christ may dwell in your hearts through faith; that you, being rooted and grounded in love, may have power to comprehend with all the saints what is the breadth and length and height and depth, and to know the love of Christ which surpasses knowledge, that you may be filled with all the fullness of God.

Ephesians 3:14–19

You shall receive power when the Holy Spirit has come upon you.

Acts 1:8

ABIDE IN CHRIST

Abide in me, and I in you. As the branch cannot bear fruit by itself, unless it abides in the vine, neither can you, unless you abide in me. I am the vine, you are the branches. He who abides in me, and I in him, he it is that bears much fruit, for apart from me you can do nothing . . . If you abide in me, and my words abide in you, ask whatever you will, and it shall be done for you.

John 15:4–5, 7

The anointing which you received from him abides in you, and you have no need that any one should teach you; as his anointing teaches you about everything, and is true, and is no lie, just as it has taught you, abide in him.

1 John 2:27

Jesus said to those Jews who believed Him, "If you abide in My word, you are My disciples indeed."

John 8:31(NKJV)

HUNGER FOR RIGHTEOUSNESS

Blessed are those who hunger and thirst for righteousness, for they will be filled.

Matthew 5:6 (NIV)

Oh, that men would give thanks to the Lord for His goodness, and for His wonderful works to the children of men! For He satisfies the longing soul, and fills the hungry soul with goodness.

Psalm 107:8–9 (NKJV)

He has filled the hungry with good things but has sent the rich away empty.

Luke 1:53 (NIV)

Him we preach, warning every man and teaching every man in all wisdom, that we may present every man perfect in Christ Jesus. To this end I also labor, striving according to His working which works in me mightily.

Colossians 1:28–29 (NKJV)

Therefore, leaving the discussion of the elementary principles of Christ, let us go on to perfection, not laying again the foundation of repentance from dead works and of faith toward God.

Hebrews 6:1 (NKJV)

Put on then, as God's chosen ones, holy and beloved, compassion, kindness, lowliness, meekness, and patience, forbearing one another and, if one has a complaint against another, forgiving each other; as the Lord has forgiven you, so you also must forgive. And above all these put on love, which binds everything together in perfect harmony.

Colossians 3:12–14

UNITED WE STAND

How good and pleasant it is when God's people live together in unity!

Psalm 133:1 (NIV)

[Be] eager to maintain the unity of the Spirit in the bond of peace . . . until we all attain to the unity of the faith and of the knowledge of the Son of God, to mature manhood, to the measure of the stature of the fulness of Christ.

Ephesians 4:3, 13

Knowing their thoughts, he said to them, "Every kingdom divided against itself is laid waste, and no city or house divided against itself will stand."

Matthew 12:25

SHOW YOUR FAITH

Now faith is the substance of things hoped for, the evidence of things not seen . . . But without faith it is impossible to please Him, for he who comes to God must believe that He is, and that He is a rewarder of those who diligently seek Him.

Hebrews 11:1, 6 (NKJV)

Whatever is born of God overcomes the world. And this is the victory that has overcome the world—our faith.

1 John 5:4 (NKJV)

So faith by itself, if it has no works, is dead. But some one will say, "You have faith and I have works." Show me your faith apart from your works, and I by my works will show you my faith.

James 2:17–18

IF GOD WILLS

You do not know about tomorrow. What is your life? For you are a mist that appears for a little time and then vanishes. Instead you ought to say, "If the Lord wills, we shall live and we shall do this or that."

James 4:14–15

When they asked him to stay for a longer period, he declined; but on taking leave of them he said, "I will return to you if God wills."

Acts 18:20–21

This we will do if God permits.

Hebrews 6:3

DON'T BE AFRAID

Say to those with fearful hearts, "Be strong, do not fear; your God will come, he will come with vengeance; with divine retribution he will come to save you."

Isaiah 35:4 (NIV)

I, the Lord your God, hold your right hand; It is I who say to you, "Fear not, I will help you."

Isaiah 41:13

Jesus immediately said to them: "Take courage! It is I. Don't be afraid."

Matthew 14:27 (NIV)

USE YOUR TALENTS

To one he gave five talents, to another two, to another one, to each according to his ability. Then he went away. He who had received the five talents went at once and traded with them; and he made five talents more. So also, he who had the two talents made two talents more.

Matthew 25:15–17

A man's gift makes room for him, and brings him before great men.

Proverbs 18:16

Do not neglect your gift.

1 Timothy 4:14 (NIV)

HOLY, HOLY, HOLY

In the year that King Uzziah died I saw the Lord sitting upon a throne, high and lifted up; and his train filled the temple. Above him stood the seraphim; each had six wings: with two he covered his face, and with two he covered his feet, and with two he flew. And one called to another and said: "Holy, holy, holy is the Lord of hosts; the whole earth is full of his glory."

Isaiah 6:1–3

As he who called you is holy, be holy yourselves in all your conduct; since it is written, "You shall be holy, for I am holy."
1 Peter 1:15–16

The four living creatures, each of them with six wings, are full of eyes all round and within, and day and night they never cease to sing, "Holy, holy, holy, is the Lord God Almighty, who was and is and is to come!"

Revelation 4:8

CHRIST MUST INCREASE

[Christ] must increase, but I must decrease. He who comes from above is above all; he who is of the earth belongs to the earth, and of the earth he speaks; he who comes from heaven is above all.

John 3:30–31

And I, when I [Jesus] am lifted up from the earth, will draw all men to myself.

John 12:32

Being found in appearance as a man, [Jesus] humbled Himself and became obedient to the point of death, even the death of the cross. Therefore God also has highly exalted Him and given Him the name which is above every name, that at the name of Jesus every knee should bow, of those in heaven, and of those on earth, and of those under the earth, and that every tongue should confess that Jesus Christ is Lord, to the glory of God the Father.

Philippians 2:8–11 (NKJV)

CALL TO GOD

Call to me and I will answer you, and will tell you great and hidden things which you have not known.

Jeremiah 33:3

Call upon Me in the day of trouble; I will deliver you, and you shall glorify Me.

Psalm 50:15 (NKJV)

When he calls to me, I will answer him; I will be with him in trouble, I will rescue him and honor him.

Psalm 91:15

SEIZE THE DAY

This is the day which the Lord has made; let us rejoice and be glad in it.

Psalm 118:24

Be very careful, then, how you live—not as unwise but as wise, making the most of every opportunity.

Ephesians 5:15–16 (NIV)

Exhort one another every day, as long as it is called "today," that none of you may be hardened by the deceitfulness of sin. For we share in Christ, if only we hold our first confidence firm to the end.

Hebrews 3:13–14

WATCH YOUR LANGUAGE

Let your conversation be always full of grace, seasoned with salt, so that you may know how to answer everyone.

Colossians 4:6 (NIV)

He who guards his mouth preserves his life; he who opens wide his lips comes to ruin.

Proverbs 13:3

Keep your tongue from evil, and your lips from speaking deceit.

Psalm 34:13

OWE NO ONE

Owe no one anything, except to love one another; for he who loves his neighbor has fulfilled the law.

Romans 13:8

The rich rule over the poor, and the borrower is slave to the lender.

Proverbs 22:7 (NIV)

The wicked borrow and do not repay, but the righteous give generously.

Psalm 37:21 (NIV)

PRAY WITHOUT CEASING

Pray without ceasing.

1 Thessalonians 5:17 (KJV)

Pray at all times in the Spirit, with all prayer and supplication. To that end keep alert with all perseverance, making supplication for all the saints.

Ephesians 6:18

The effective, fervent prayer of a righteous man avails much.

James 5:16 (NKJV)

ATTITUDE IS EVERYTHING

Let this mind be in you which was also in Christ Jesus, who, being in the form of God, did not consider it robbery to be equal with God, but made Himself of no reputation, taking the form of a bondservant, and coming in the likeness of men. And being found in appearance as a man, He humbled Himself and became obedient to the point of death, even the death of the cross.

Philippians 2:5–8 (NKJV)

Do all things without complaining and disputing, that you may become blameless and harmless, children of God without fault in the midst of a crooked and perverse generation, among whom you shine as lights in the world.

Philippians 2:14–15 (NKJV)

In every thing give thanks: for this is the will of God in Christ Jesus concerning you.

1 Thessalonians 5:18 (KJV)

GOD IS LOVE

Beloved, let us love one another; for love is of God, and he who loves is born of God and knows God. He who does not love does not know God; for God is love.

1 John 4:7–8

A new commandment I give to you, that you love one another; even as I have loved you, that you also love one another. By this all men will know that you are my disciples, if you have love for one another.

John 13:34–35

We know and believe the love God has for us. God is love, and he who abides in love abides in God, and God abides in him.

1 John 4:16

PREACH THE WORD

Preach the word; be prepared in season and out of season; correct, rebuke and encourage—with great patience and careful instruction.

2 Timothy 4:2 (NIV)

How are men to call upon him in whom they have not believed? And how are they to believe in him of whom they have never heard? And how are they to hear without a preacher? And how can men preach unless they are sent? As it is written, "How beautiful are the feet of those who preach good news!"

Romans 10:14–15

If I preach the gospel, that gives me no ground for boasting. For necessity is laid upon me. Woe to me if I do not preach the gospel!

1 Corinthians 9:16

SET YOUR GOALS

We make it our goal to please him, whether we are at home in the body or away from it.

2 Corinthians 5:9 (NIV)

My goal is that they may be encouraged in heart and united in love, so that they may have the full riches of complete understanding, in order that they may know the mystery of God, namely, Christ.

Colossians 2:2 (NIV)

Not that I have already obtained all this, or have already arrived at my goal, but I press on to take hold of that for which Christ Jesus took hold of me. Brothers and sisters, I do not consider myself yet to have taken hold of it. But one thing I do: Forgetting what is behind and straining toward what is ahead, I press on toward the goal to win the prize for which God has called me heavenward in Christ Jesus.

Philippians 3:12–14 (NIV)

IRON SHARPENS IRON

Iron sharpens iron, and one man sharpens another.

Proverbs 27:17

Two are better than one, because they have a good return for their labor: If either of them falls down, one can help the other up. But pity anyone who falls and has no one to help them up.

Ecclesiastes 4:9–10 (NIV)

If any one refuses to obey what we say in this letter, note that man, and have nothing to do with him, that he may be ashamed. Do not look on him as an enemy, but warn him as a brother.

2 Thessalonians 3:14–15

DON'T BE STUBBORN

Listen to me, you stubborn-hearted, you who are now far from my righteousness. I am bringing my righteousness near, it is not far away; and my salvation will not be delayed. I will grant salvation to Zion, my splendor to Israel.

Isaiah 46:12–13 (NIV)

They shall say to the elders of his city, "This our son is stubborn and rebellious, he will not obey our voice; he is a glutton and a drunkard." Then all the men of the city shall stone him to death with stones; so you shall purge the evil from your midst; and all Israel shall hear, and fear.

Deuteronomy 21:20–21

The people to whom I am sending you are obstinate and stubborn. Say to them, "This is what the Sovereign Lord says." And whether they listen or fail to listen—for they are a rebellious people—they will know that a prophet has been among them.

Ezekiel 2:4–5 (NIV)

COMMIT YOUR WAY

Commit your way to the Lord, trust also in Him, and He shall bring it to pass.

Psalm 37:5 (NKJV)

You therefore, my son, be strong in the grace that is in Christ Jesus. And the things that you have heard from me among many witnesses, commit these to faithful men who will be able to teach others also.

2 Timothy 2:1–2 (NKJV)

Commit your work to the Lord, and your plans will be established.

Proverbs 16:3

BE FULLY PERSUADED

[Abraham] staggered not at the promise of God through unbelief; but was strong in faith, giving glory to God; and being fully persuaded that, what he had promised, he was able also to perform.

Romans 4:20–21 (KJV)

I am not ashamed: for I know whom I have believed, and am persuaded that he is able to keep that which I have committed unto him against that day.

2 Timothy 1:12 (KJV)

Let us hold fast the confession of our hope without wavering, for he who promised is faithful.

Hebrews 10:23

DON'T UNDERESTIMATE YOUTH

Let no one despise your youth, but set the believers an example in speech and conduct, in love, in faith, in purity.

1 Timothy 4:12

[Jeremiah] said, "Ah, Lord God! Behold, I do not know how to speak, for I am only a youth." But the Lord said to me, "Do not say, 'I am only a youth'; for to all to whom I send you you shall go, and whatever I command you you shall speak. Be not afraid of them, for I am with you to deliver you, says the Lord."

Jeremiah 1:6–8

When the Philistine looked, and saw David, he disdained him; for he was but a youth, ruddy and comely in appearance . . . And David put his hand in his bag and took out a stone, and slung it, and struck the Philistine on his forehead; the stone sank into his forehead, and he fell on his face to the ground.

1 Samuel 17:42, 49

GOD'S GRACE SUFFICES

[The Lord] said to me, "My grace is sufficient for you, for my power is made perfect in weakness." I will all the more gladly boast of my weaknesses, that the power of Christ may rest upon me. For the sake of Christ, then, I am content with weaknesses, insults, hardships, persecutions, and calamities; for when I am weak, then I am strong.

2 Corinthians 12:9–10

Not that we are sufficient of ourselves to think of anything as being from ourselves, but our sufficiency is from God.

2 Corinthians 3:5 (NKJV)

God is able to make all grace abound toward you, that you, always having all sufficiency in all things, may have an abundance for every good work.

2 Corinthians 9:8 (NKJV)

LEND A HAND

The poor will never cease out of the land; therefore I command you, You shall open wide your hand to your brother, to the needy and to the poor, in the land.

Deuteronomy 15:11

Whoever is kind to the poor lends to the Lord, and he will reward them for what they have done.

Proverbs 19:17 (NIV)

She opens her arms to the poor and extends her hands to the needy.

Proverbs 31:20 (NIV)

SPEND TIME WISELY

Conduct yourselves wisely toward outsiders, making the most of the time.

Colossians 4:5

The Lord looks down from heaven upon the children of men, to see if there are any that act wisely, that seek after God.

Psalm 14:2

Come now, you who say, "Today or tomorrow we will go into such and such a town and spend a year there and trade and get gain"; whereas you do not know about to-morrow. What is your life? For you are a mist that appears for a little time and then vanishes.

James 4:13–14

TIME WILL HEAL

For everything there is a season, and a time for every matter under heaven: a time to be born, and a time to die; a time to plant, and a time to pluck up what is planted; a time to kill, and a time to heal; a time to break down, and a time to build up; a time to weep, and a time to laugh; a time to mourn, and a time to dance.

Ecclesiastes 3:1–4

Then shall your light break forth like the dawn, and your healing shall spring up speedily; your righteousness shall go before you, the glory of the Lord shall be your rear guard.

Isaiah 58:8

Praise the Lord. How good is it to sing praises to our God, how pleasant and fitting to praise him! . . . He heals the brokenhearted and binds up their wounds.

Psalm 147:1, 3 (NIV)

DO UNTO OTHERS

In everything, do to others what you would have them do to you, for this sums up the Law and the Prophets.

Matthew 7:12 (NIV)

The whole law is fulfilled in one word, "You shall love your neighbor as yourself."

Galatians 5:14

Do to others as you would have them do to you.

Luke 6:31 (NIV)

JUDGE NO ONE

Do not judge, or you too will be judged. For in the same way you judge others, you will be judged, and with the measure you use, it will be measured to you.

Matthew 7:1–2 (NIV)

Judge not, and you will not be judged; condemn not, and you will not be condemned; forgive, and you will be forgiven.

Luke 6:37

Let us not judge one another anymore, but rather resolve this, not to put a stumbling block or a cause to fall in our brother's way.

Romans 14:13 (NKJV)

SEEK HIM EARLY

O God, You are my God; early will I seek You; my soul thirsts for You; my flesh longs for You in a dry and thirsty land where there is no water.

Psalm 63:1 (NKJV)

The steadfast love of the Lord never ceases, his mercies never come to an end; they are new every morning; great is thy faithfulness.

Lamentations 3:22–23

The Lord is righteous in her midst, He will do no unrighteousness. Every morning He brings His justice to light; He never fails.

Zephaniah 3:5 (NKJV)

LAUGH OUT LOUD

A merry heart does good, like medicine, but a broken spirit dries the bones.

Proverbs 17:22 (NKJV)

For everything there is a season, and a time for every matter under heaven: . . . a time to weep, and a time to laugh.

Ecclesiastes 3:1, 4

Sarah said, "God has brought me laughter, and everyone who hears about this will laugh with me."

Genesis 21:6 (NIV)

JESUS LOVES ME

As the Father has loved me, so have I loved you; abide in my love . . . This is my commandment, that you love one another as I have loved you. Greater love has no man than this, that a man lay down his life for his friends.

John 15:9, 12–13

For God so loved the world that he gave his only Son, that whoever believes in him should not perish but have eternal life.

John 3:16

I have been crucified with Christ and I no longer live, but Christ lives in me. The life I now live in the body, I live by faith in the Son of God, who loved me and gave himself for me.

Galatians 2:20 (NIV)

LOVE YOUR ENEMIES

You have heard that it was said, "Love your neighbor and hate your enemy." But I tell you, love your enemies and pray for those who persecute you.

Matthew 5:43–44 (NIV)

If your enemy is hungry, give him bread to eat; and if he is thirsty, give him water to drink.

Proverbs 25:21

Love your enemies, and do good, and lend, expecting nothing in return; and your reward will be great, and you will be sons of the Most High; for he is kind to the ungrateful and the selfish. Be merciful, even as your Father is merciful.

Luke 6:35–36

THIS SHALL PASS

Heaven and earth will pass away, but my words will not pass away.

Matthew 24:35

Now listen, you who say, "Today or tomorrow we will go to this or that city, spend a year there, carry on business and make money." Why, you do not even know what will happen tomorrow. What is your life? You are a mist that appears for a little while and then vanishes.

James 4:13–14 (NIV)

The world passes away, and the lust of it; but he who does the will of God abides for ever.

1 John 2:17

PUT AWAY IDOLS

Little children, keep yourselves from idols. Amen.

1 John 5:21 (KJV)

You shall have no other gods before Me. You shall not make for yourself a carved image—any likeness of anything that is in heaven above, or that is in the earth beneath, or that is in the water under the earth; you shall not bow down to them nor serve them. For I, the Lord your God, am a jealous God, visiting the iniquity of the fathers upon the children to the third and fourth generations of those who hate Me.

Exodus 20:3–5 (NKJV)

My dear friends, flee from idolatry.

1 Corinthians 10:14 (NIV)

KEEP YOURSELF HUMBLE

Humble yourselves therefore under the mighty hand of God, that he may exalt you in due time.

1 Peter 5:6 (KJV)

For thus says the high and lofty One who inhabits eternity, whose name is Holy: "I dwell in the high and holy place, and also with him who is of a contrite and humble spirit, to revive the spirit of the humble, and to revive the heart of the contrite."

Isaiah 57:15

Humble yourselves in the sight of the Lord, and he shall lift you up.

James 4:10 (KJV)

FORGIVE THEIR TRESPASSES

Forgive us our debts, as we forgive our debtors.

Matthew 6:12 (KJV)

If you forgive men their trespasses, your heavenly Father also will forgive you; but if you do not forgive men their trespasses, neither will your Father forgive your trespasses.

Matthew 6:14–15

Peter came up and said to him, "Lord, how often shall my brother sin against me, and I forgive him? As many as seven times?" Jesus said to him, "I do not say to you seven times, but seventy times seven."

Matthew 18:21–22

JESUS WILL RETURN

Do not let your hearts be troubled. You believe in God; believe also in me. My Father's house has many rooms; if that were not so, would I have told you that I am going there to prepare a place for you? And if I go and prepare a place for you, I will come back and take you to be with me that you also may be where I am.

John 14:1–3 (NIV)

You heard me say, "I am going away and I am coming back to you." If you loved me, you would be glad that I am going to the Father, for the Father is greater than I.

John 14:28 (NIV)

He who testifies to these things says, "Surely I am coming quickly." Amen. Even so, come, Lord Jesus!

Revelation 22:20 (NKJV)

FATHER KNOWS BEST

But you, do not be called "Rabbi"; for One is your Teacher, the Christ, and you are all brethren. Do not call anyone on earth your father; for One is your Father, He who is in heaven.

Matthew 23:8–9 (NKJV)

For I know the plans I have for you, says the Lord, plans for welfare and not for evil, to give you a future and a hope.

Jeremiah 29:11

Your Father knows the things you have need of before you ask Him.

Matthew 6:8 (NKJV)

GOD DOESN'T CHANGE

I am the Lord, I do not change.

Malachi 3:6 (NKJV)

Every good gift and every perfect gift is from above, and comes down from the Father of lights, with whom there is no variation or shadow of turning.

James 1:17 (NKJV)

Jesus Christ is the same yesterday, today, and forever.

Hebrews 13:8 (NKJV)

CHERISH YOUR MEMORIES

Mary treasured up all these things and pondered them in her heart.

Luke 2:19 (NIV)

I thank my God upon every remembrance of you.

Philippians 1:3 (KJV)

Oh, give thanks to the Lord! . . . Remember His marvelous works which He has done.

1 Chronicles 16:8, 12 (NKJV)

DARE TO DREAM

Where there is no vision, the people perish.

Proverbs 29:18 (KJV)

He said, "Hear my words: If there is a prophet among you, I the Lord make myself known to him in a vision, I speak with him in a dream."

Numbers 12:6

In the last days it shall be, God declares, that I will pour out my Spirit upon all flesh, and your sons and your daughters shall prophesy, and your young men shall see visions, and your old men shall dream dreams.

Acts 2:17

GOD IS FAITHFUL

Know therefore that the Lord your God is God; he is the faithful God, keeping his covenant of love to a thousand generations of those who love him and keep his commandments.

Deuteronomy 7:9 (NIV)

God is faithful, who has called you into fellowship with his Son, Jesus Christ our Lord.

1 Corinthians 1:9 (NIV)

Let us hold fast the confession of our hope without wavering, for he who promised is faithful.

Hebrews 10:23

LIGHT YOUR WORLD

You are the light of the world. A city set on a hill cannot be hid.

Matthew 5:14

Jesus spoke to them, saying, "I am the light of the world; he who follows me will not walk in darkness, but will have the light of life."

John 8:12

Do all things without grumbling or questioning, that you may be blameless and innocent, children of God without blemish in the midst of a crooked and perverse generation, among whom you shine as lights in the world.

Philippians 2:14–15

Having gifts that differ according to the grace given to us, let us use them: if prophecy, in proportion to our faith; if service, in our serving; he who teaches, in his teaching.

Romans 12:6–7

God has placed in the church first of all apostles, second prophets, third teachers, then miracles, then gifts of healing, of helping, of guidance, and of different kinds of tongues.

1 Corinthians 12:28 (NIV)

His gifts were that some should be apostles, some prophets, some evangelists, some pastors and teachers, to equip the saints for the work of ministry, for building up the body of Christ.

Ephesians 4:11–12

LOVE YOUR SPOUSE

"**A** man shall leave his father and mother and be joined to his wife, and the two shall become one flesh." This mystery is a profound one, and I am saying that it refers to Christ and the church; however, let each one of you love his wife as himself, and let the wife see that she respects her husband.

Ephesians 5:31–33

Husbands, in the same way be considerate as you live with your wives, and treat them with respect as the weaker partner and as heirs with you of the gracious gift of life, so that nothing will hinder your prayers.

1 Peter 3:7 (NIV)

A good wife who can find? She is far more precious than jewels. The heart of her husband trusts in her, and he will have no lack of gain.

Proverbs 31:10–11

HOPE SPRINGS ETERNAL

You are my hope, O Lord God; You are my trust from my youth.

Psalm 71:5 (NKJV)

Hope does not disappoint us, because God's love has been poured into our hearts through the Holy Spirit which has been given to us.

Romans 5:5

Not only the creation, but we ourselves, who have the first fruits of the Spirit, groan inwardly as we wait for adoption as sons, the redemption of our bodies. For in this hope we were saved. Now hope that is seen is not hope. For who hopes for what he sees? But if we hope for what we do not see, we wait for it with patience.

Romans 8:23–25

OBEY YOUR PARENTS

Children, obey your parents in the Lord, for this is right.

Ephesians 6:1

My son, keep your father's command and do not forsake your mother's teaching.

Proverbs 6:20 (NIV)

Children, obey your parents in everything, for this pleases the Lord.

Colossians 3:20

SAY YOUR PRAYERS

I exhort therefore, that, first of all, supplications, prayers, intercessions, and giving of thanks, be made for all men; for kings, and for all that are in authority; that we may lead a quiet and peaceable life in all godliness and honesty.

1 Timothy 2:1–2 (KJV)

I cry with my voice to the Lord, with my voice I make supplication to the Lord, I pour out my complaint before him, I tell my trouble before him.

Psalm 142:1–2

The eyes of the Lord are upon the righteous, and his ears are open to their prayer.

1 Peter 3:12

ASK, SEEK, KNOCK

Ask, and it will be given you; seek, and you will find; knock, and it will be opened to you. For every one who asks receives, and he who seeks finds, and to him who knocks it will be opened.

Matthew 7:7–8

Seek the Lord while he may be found; call on him while he is near.

Isaiah 55:6 (NIV)

You do not have, because you do not ask.

James 4:2

TRAIN A CHILD

Train up a child in the way he should go, and when he is old he will not depart from it.

Proverbs 22:6

Do not withhold discipline from a child.

Proverbs 23:13 (NIV)

You shall love the Lord your God with all your heart, and with all your soul, and with all your might. And these words which I command you this day shall be upon your heart; and you shall teach them diligently to your children, and shall talk of them when you sit in your house, and when you walk by the way, and when you lie down, and when you rise. And you shall bind them as a sign upon your hand, and they shall be as frontlets between your eyes. And you shall write them on the doorposts of your house and on your gates.

Deuteronomy 6:5–9

READ TO SUCCEED

Search from the book of the Lord, and read: not one of these shall fail.

Isaiah 34:16 (NKJV)

This book of the law shall not depart out of your mouth, but you shall meditate on it day and night, that you may be careful to do according to all that is written in it; for then you shall make your way prosperous, and then you shall have good success.

Joshua 1:8

If the ax is dull, and one does not sharpen the edge, then he must use more strength; but wisdom brings success.

Ecclesiastes 10:10 (NKJV)

PUT OTHERS FIRST

Do nothing out of selfish ambition or vain conceit. Rather, in humility value others above yourselves, not looking to your own interests but each of you to the interests of the others.

Philippians 2:3–4 (NIV)

Love your neighbor as yourself.

Mark 12:31 (NIV)

Let no one seek his own, but each one the other's well-being.

1 Corinthians 10:24 (NKJV)

EXPECT THE UNEXPECTED

My soul, wait silently for God alone, for my expectation is from Him.

Psalm 62:5 (NKJV)

You also must be ready; for the Son of man is coming at an unexpected hour.

Luke 12:40

I know that this will turn out for my deliverance through your prayer and the supply of the Spirit of Jesus Christ, according to my earnest expectation and hope that in nothing I shall be ashamed.

Philippians 1:19–20 (NKJV)

PRESERVE GOD'S WORD

These words which I command you this day shall be upon your heart; and you shall teach them diligently to your children, and shall talk of them when you sit in your house, and when you walk by the way, and when you lie down, and when you rise.

Deuteronomy 6:6–7

When he sits on the throne of his kingdom, he shall write for himself in a book a copy of this law, from that which is in charge of the Levitical priests; and it shall be with him, and he shall read in it all the days of his life, that he may learn to fear the Lord his God, by keeping all the words of this law and these statutes, and doing them.

Deuteronomy 17:18–19

This is what the Lord, the God of Israel, says: "Write in a book all the words I have spoken to you."

Jeremiah 30:2 (NIV)

SAVED BY GRACE

By grace you have been saved through faith, and that not of yourselves; it is the gift of God.

Ephesians 2:8 (NKJV)

Do not be ashamed then of testifying to our Lord, nor of me his prisoner, but share in suffering for the gospel in the power of God, who saved us and called us with a holy calling, not in virtue of our works but in virtue of his own purpose and the grace which he gave us in Christ Jesus ages ago.

2 Timothy 1:8–9

If, because of one man's trespass, death reigned through that one man, much more will those who receive the abundance of grace and the free gift of righteousness reign in life through the one man Jesus Christ.

Romans 5:17

NUMBER YOUR DAYS

Teach us to number our days, that we may gain a heart of wisdom.

Psalm 90:12 (NIV)

A person's days are determined; you have decreed the number of his months and have set limits he cannot exceed.

Job 14:5 (NIV)

Show me, Lord, my life's end and the number of my days; let me know how fleeting my life is.

Psalm 39:4 (NIV)

GOD IS GREAT

Great is the Lord, and greatly to be praised, and he is to be held in awe above all gods.

1 Chronicles 16:25

The Lord your God is God of gods and Lord of lords, the great God, mighty and awesome, who shows no partiality and accepts no bribes.

Deuteronomy 10:17 (NIV)

Praise the Lord, my soul. Lord my God, you are very great; you are clothed with splendor and majesty.

Psalm 104:1 (NIV)

ENJOY YOUR LIFE

As for the rich in this world, charge them not to be haughty, nor to set their hopes on uncertain riches but on God who richly furnishes us with everything to enjoy.

1 Timothy 6:17

Nothing is better for a man than that he should eat and drink, and that his soul should enjoy good in his labor. This also, I saw, was from the hand of God.

Ecclesiastes 2:24 (NKJV)

Until now you have asked nothing in My name. Ask, and you will receive, that your joy may be full.

John 16:24 (NKJV)

CHILDREN ARE GIFTS

Lo, children are an heritage of the Lord: and the fruit of the womb is his reward.

Psalm 127:3 (KJV)

Blessed is every one who fears the Lord, who walks in His ways . . . Your wife shall be like a fruitful vine in the very heart of your house, your children like olive plants all around your table . . . Yes, may you see your children's children.

Psalm 128:1, 3, 6 (NKJV)

Every good and perfect gift is from above, coming down from the Father of the heavenly lights.

James 1:17 (NIV)

GLORY TO GOD

As each has received a gift, employ it for one another, as good stewards of God's varied grace: whoever speaks, as one who utters oracles of God; whoever renders service, as one who renders it by the strength which God supplies; in order that in everything God may be glorified through Jesus Christ. To him belong glory and dominion for ever and ever. Amen.

1 Peter 4:10–11

Give to the Lord, O families of the peoples, give to the Lord glory and strength. Give to the Lord the glory due His name; bring an offering, and come before Him. Oh, worship the Lord in the beauty of holiness!

1 Chronicles 16:28–29 (NKJV)

You are worthy, our Lord and God, to receive glory and honor and power, for you created all things, and by your will they were created and have their being.

Revelation 4:11 (NIV)

LORD, SEND ME

I heard the voice of the Lord, saying: Whom shall I send, and who will go for us? Then said I, Here am I; Send me.

Isaiah 6:8 (KJV)

[Jesus] said to his disciples, "The harvest is plentiful, but the laborers are few; pray therefore the Lord of the harvest to send out laborers into his harvest."

Matthew 9:37–38

Jesus said to them again, "Peace be with you. As the Father has sent me, even so I send you."

John 20:21

PLEASE PAY ATTENTION

My son, give attention to my words; incline your ear to my sayings. Do not let them depart from your eyes; keep them in the midst of your heart; for they are life to those who find them, and health to all their flesh.

Proverbs 4:20–22 (NKJV)

Be sober, be watchful. Your adversary the devil prowls around like a roaring lion, seeking some one to devour.

1 Peter 5:8

Till I come, give attention to reading, to exhortation, to doctrine.

1 Timothy 4:13 (NKJV)

GOD'S AT WORK

We know that in all things God works for the good of those who love him, who have been called according to his purpose.

Romans 8:28 (NIV)

Joseph said to them, "Do not be afraid, for am I in the place of God? But as for you, you meant evil against me; but God meant it for good, in order to bring it about as it is this day, to save many people alive.

Genesis 50:19–20 (NKJV)

O Lord, how manifold are Your works! In wisdom You have made them all. The earth is full of Your possessions.

Psalm 104:24 (NKJV)

LOVE NEVER FAILS

Whoever confesses that Jesus is the Son of God, God abides in him, and he in God. So we know and believe the love God has for us. God is love, and he who abides in love abides in God, and God abides in him.

1 John 4:15–16

Love never fails.

1 Corinthians 13:8 (NIV)

Be strong and of a good courage, fear not, nor be afraid of them: for the Lord thy God, he it is that doth go with thee; he will not fail thee, nor forsake thee.

Deuteronomy 31:6 (KJV)

BELIEVE AND RECEIVE

Whatever things you ask in prayer, believing, you will receive.

Matthew 21:22 (NKJV)

When you ask, you must believe and not doubt, because the one who doubts is like a wave of the sea, blown and tossed by the wind. That person should not expect to receive anything from the Lord.

James 1:6–7 (NIV)

Whatever things you ask when you pray, believe that you receive them, and you will have them.

Mark 11:24 (NKJV)

DO YOUR HOMEWORK

He who looks into the perfect law of liberty and continues in it, and is not a forgetful hearer but a doer of the work, this one will be blessed in what he does.

James 1:25 (NKJV)

Prepare your outside work, make it fit for yourself in the field; and afterward build your house.

Proverbs 24:27 (NKJV)

Study to show thyself approved unto God, a workman that needeth not to be ashamed, rightly dividing the word of truth.

2 Timothy 2:15 (KJV)

FAMILIARITY BREEDS CONTEMPT

Jesus himself testified that a prophet has no honor in his own country.

John 4:44

He was in the world, and though the world was made through him, the world did not recognize him. He came to that which was his own, but his own did not receive him.

John 1:10–11 (NIV)

Many of them that sleep in the dust of the earth shall awake, some to everlasting life, and some to shame and everlasting contempt.

Daniel 12:2 (KJV)

HEAR GOD'S WORD

Faith comes by hearing, and hearing by the word of God.
Romans 10:17 (NKJV)

[Jesus] said to them, "Take heed what you hear; the measure you give will be the measure you get, and still more will be given you."

Mark 4:24

He who received the seed on stony places, this is he who hears the word and immediately receives it with joy; yet he has no root in himself, but endures only for a while. For when tribulation or persecution arises because of the word, immediately he stumbles. Now he who received seed among the thorns is he who hears the word, and the cares of this world and the deceitfulness of riches choke the word, and he becomes unfruitful.

Matthew 13:20–22 (NKJV)

ALWAYS GIVE THANKS

Sing and make music from your heart to the Lord, always giving thanks to God the Father for everything, in the name of our Lord Jesus Christ.

Ephesians 5:19–20 (NIV)

We give thanks to God always for you all, constantly mentioning you in our prayers.

1 Thessalonians 1:2

Give thanks in all circumstances; for this is the will of God in Christ Jesus for you.

1 Thessalonians 5:18

DRESS FOR SUCCESS

I also want the women to dress modestly, with decency and propriety, adorning themselves, not with elaborate hairstyles or gold or pearls or expensive clothes, but with good deeds, appropriate for women who profess to worship God.

1 Timothy 2:9–10 (NIV)

Do not let your adornment be merely outward—arranging the hair, wearing gold, or putting on fine apparel—rather let it be the hidden person of the heart, with the incorruptible beauty of a gentle and quiet spirit, which is very precious in the sight of God.

1 Peter 3:3–4 (NKJV)

Let Your priests be clothed with righteousness, and let Your saints shout for joy . . . I will also clothe [Zion's] priests with salvation, and her saints shall shout aloud for joy.

Psalm 132:9, 16 (NKJV)

DO NOT STEAL

You shall not steal.

Exodus 20:15 (NIV)

You, therefore, who teach another, do you not teach yourself? You who preach that a man should not steal, do you steal?

Romans 2:21 (NKJV)

Let him who stole steal no longer, but rather let him labor, working with his hands what is good, that he may have something to give him who has need.

Ephesians 4:28 (NKJV)

COUNT THE COST

Which of you, intending to build a tower, does not sit down first and count the cost, whether he has enough to finish it . . . So likewise, whoever of you does not forsake all that he has cannot be My disciple.

Luke 14:28, 33 (NKJV)

Whatever gain I had, I counted as loss for the sake of Christ. Indeed I count everything as loss because of the surpassing worth of knowing Christ Jesus my Lord. For his sake I have suffered the loss of all things, and count them as refuse, in order that I may gain Christ.

Philippians 3:7–8

The kingdom of heaven is like a merchant in search of fine pearls, who, on finding one pearl of great value, went and sold all that he had and bought it.

Matthew 13:45–46

BEHOLD THE LAMB

The next day he saw Jesus coming toward him, and said, "Behold, the Lamb of God, who takes away the sin of the world!"

John 1:29

He was oppressed and He was afflicted, yet He opened not His mouth; He was led as a lamb to the slaughter, and as a sheep before its shearers is silent, so He opened not His mouth.

Isaiah 53:7 (NKJV)

Then I looked, and I heard the voice of many angels around the throne, the living creatures, and the elders; and the number of them was ten thousand times ten thousand, and thousands of thousands, saying with a loud voice: "Worthy is the Lamb who was slain to receive power and riches and wisdom, and strength and honor and glory and blessing!"

Revelation 5:11–12 (NKJV)

ACCENTUATE THE POSITIVE

Finally, brethren, whatever things are true, whatever things are noble, whatever things are just, whatever things are pure, whatever things are lovely, whatever things are of good report, if there is any virtue and if there is anything praiseworthy—meditate on these things.

Philippians 4:8 (NKJV)

We know that all things work together for good to them that love God, to them who are the called according to his purpose.

Romans 8:28 (KJV)

The good man out of his good treasure brings forth good, and the evil man out of his evil treasure brings forth evil. I tell you, on the day of judgment men will render account for every careless word they utter; for by your words you will be justified, and by your words you will be condemned.

Matthew 12:35–37

BE A BLESSING

I will make of you a great nation, and I will bless you, and make your name great, so that you will be a blessing.

Genesis 12:2

Finally, all of you be of one mind, having compassion for one another; love as brothers, be tenderhearted, be courteous; not returning evil for evil or reviling for reviling, but on the contrary blessing, knowing that you were called to this, that you may inherit a blessing.

1 Peter 3:8–9 (NKJV)

I say to you, love your enemies, bless those who curse you, do good to those who hate you, and pray for those who spitefully use you and persecute you.

Matthew 5:44 (NKJV)

CHANGE THE WORLD

Do not love the world or the things in the world. If any one loves the world, love for the Father is not in him. For all that is in the world, the lust of the flesh and the lust of the eyes and the pride of life, is not of the Father but is of the world. And the world passes away, and the lust of it; but he who does the will of God abides for ever.

1 John 2:15–17

Do not be conformed to this world, but be transformed by the renewing of your mind, that you may prove what is that good and acceptable and perfect will of God.

Romans 12:2 (NKJV)

[Jesus] said to them, "Go into all the world and preach the gospel to all creation. Whoever believes and is baptized will be saved, but whoever does not believe will be condemned."

Mark 16:15–16 (NIV)

HOME SWEET HOME

If the earthly tent we live in is destroyed, we have a building from God, an eternal house in heaven, not built by human hands.

2 Corinthians 5:1 (NIV)

Jesus answered him, "If a man loves me, he will keep my word, and my Father will love him, and we will come to him and make our home with him."

John 14:23

People who speak thus make it clear that they are seeking a homeland. If they had been thinking of that land from which they had gone out, they would have had opportunity to return. But as it is, they desire a better country, that is, a heavenly one. Therefore God is not ashamed to be called their God, for he has prepared for them a city.

Hebrews 11:14–16

LEARN GODLY CONTENTMENT

Not that I speak in regard to need, for I have learned in whatever state I am, to be content: I know how to be abased, and I know how to abound. Everywhere and in all things I have learned both to be full and to be hungry, both to abound and to suffer need. I can do all things through Christ who strengthens me.

Philippians 4:11–13 (NKJV)

Give me neither poverty nor riches; feed me with the food that is needful for me, lest I be full, and deny thee, and say, "Who is the Lord?" or lest I be poor, and steal.

Proverbs 30:8–9

There is great gain in godliness with contentment; for we brought nothing into the world, and we cannot take anything out of the world; but if we have food and clothing, with these we shall be content.

1 Timothy 6:6–8

MY REDEEMER LIVES

I know that my Redeemer lives, and at last he will stand upon the earth.

Job 19:25

They remembered that God was their rock, the Most High God their redeemer.

Psalm 78:35

I am He who lives, and was dead, and behold, I am alive forevermore. Amen. And I have the keys of Hades and of Death.

Revelation 1:18 (NKJV)

RISE AND SHINE

Arise, shine; for your light has come, and the glory of the Lord has risen upon you.

Isaiah 60:1

He says: "Awake, you who sleep, arise from the dead, and Christ will give you light."

Ephesians 5:14 (NKJV)

Be blameless and innocent, children of God without blemish in the midst of a crooked and perverse generation, among whom you shine as lights in the world.

Philippians 2:15

WORDS CAN HURT

A good man out of the good treasure of his heart brings forth good things, and an evil man out of the evil treasure brings forth evil things. But I say to you that for every idle word men may speak, they will give account of it in the day of judgment. For by your words you will be justified, and by your words you will be condemned.

Matthew 12:35–37 (NKJV)

The tongue is a fire, a world of iniquity. The tongue is so set among our members that it defiles the whole body, and sets on fire the course of nature; and it is set on fire by hell . . . But no man can tame the tongue. It is an unruly evil, full of deadly poison.

James 3:6, 8 (NKJV)

Let your speech always be gracious, seasoned with salt, so that you may know how you ought to answer every one.

Colossians 4:6

REPENT FROM SIN

In those days came John the Baptist, preaching in the wilderness of Judea, "Repent, for the kingdom of heaven is at hand."

Matthew 3:1–2

Peter said to them, "Repent, and be baptized every one of you in the name of Jesus Christ for the forgiveness of your sins; and you shall receive the gift of the Holy Spirit."

Acts 2:38

The Lord is not slack concerning His promise, as some count slackness, but is longsuffering toward us, not willing that any should perish but that all should come to repentance.

2 Peter 3:9 (NKJV)

DO NOT OVEREAT

Have you found honey? Eat only as much as you need, lest you be filled with it and vomit.

Proverbs 25:16 (NKJV)

Do not join those who drink too much wine or gorge themselves on meat, for drunkards and gluttons become poor, and drowsiness clothes them in rags.

Proverbs 23:20–21 (NIV)

It is not good to eat much honey; so to seek one's own glory is not glory.

Proverbs 25:27 (NKJV)

BEST FRIENDS FOREVER

A friend loves at all times, and a brother is born for adversity.

Proverbs 17:17

A man who has friends must himself be friendly, but there is a friend who sticks closer than a brother.

Proverbs 18:24 (NKJV)

Your friend, and your father's friend, do not forsake; and do not go to your brother's house in the day of your calamity. Better is a neighbor who is near than a brother who is far away.

Proverbs 27:10

ANSWER THE CALL

Brothers and sisters, think of what you were when you were called. Not many of you were wise by human standards; not many were influential; not many were of noble birth. But God chose the foolish things of the world to shame the wise; God chose the weak things of the world to shame the strong. God chose the lowly things of this world and the despised things—and the things that are not—to nullify the things that are.

1 Corinthians 1:26–28 (NIV)

Let each one remain in the same calling in which he was called.

1 Corinthians 7:20 (NKJV)

I, therefore, a prisoner of the Lord, beg you to lead a life worthy of the calling to which you have been called.

Ephesians 4:1

TRUST THE LORD

Trust in the Lord with all your heart, and lean not on your own understanding; in all your ways acknowledge Him, and He shall direct your paths.

Proverbs 3:5–6 (NKJV)

Trust in the Lord, and do good; so you will dwell in the land, and enjoy security. Take delight in the Lord, and he will give you the desires of your heart.

Psalm 37:3–4

Lord Almighty, blessed is the one who trusts in you.

Psalm 84:12 (NIV)

WISDOM BRINGS SUCCESS

If the ax is dull, and one does not sharpen the edge, then he must use more strength; but wisdom brings success.

Ecclesiastes 10:10 (NKJV)

If any of you lacks wisdom, let him ask God, who gives to all men generously and without reproaching, and it will be given him.

James 1:5

He who gets wisdom loves himself; he who keeps understanding will prosper.

Proverbs 19:8

GIVE WITHOUT RELUCTANCE

Each of you should give what you have decided in your heart to give, not reluctantly or under compulsion, for God loves a cheerful giver. And God is able to bless you abundantly, so that in all things at all times, having all that you need, you will abound in every good work.

2 Corinthians 9:7–8 (NIV)

He who has a generous eye will be blessed, for he gives of his bread to the poor.

Proverbs 22:9 (NKJV)

The righteous considers the cause of the poor, but the wicked does not understand such knowledge.

Proverbs 29:7 (NKJV)

DON'T BE LAZY

The soul of a lazy man desires, and has nothing; but the soul of the diligent shall be made rich.

Proverbs 13:4 (NKJV)

A lazy man buries his hand in the bowl, and will not so much as bring it to his mouth again.

Proverbs 19:24 (NKJV)

I went by the field of the lazy man, and by the vineyard of the man devoid of understanding; and there it was, all overgrown with thorns; its surface was covered with nettles; its stone wall was broken down. When I saw it, I considered it well; I looked on it and received instruction: A little sleep, a little slumber, a little folding of the hands to rest; so shall your poverty come like a prowler, and your need like an armed man.

Proverbs 24:30–34 (NKJV)

PAY YOUR DUES

Pay all of them their dues, taxes to whom taxes are due, revenue to whom revenue is due, respect to whom respect is due, honor to whom honor is due.

Romans 13:7

"Should we pay [taxes], or should we not?" But knowing their hypocrisy, he said to them, "Why put me to the test? Bring me a coin, and let me look at it." And they brought one. And he said to them, "Whose likeness and inscription is this?" They said to him, "Caesar's." Jesus said to them, "Render to Caesar the things that are Caesar's, and to God the things that are God's." And they were amazed at him.

Mark 12:15–17

Let us not grow weary in well-doing, for in due season we shall reap, if we do not lose heart.

Galatians 6:9

GUARD YOUR HEART

Keep your heart with all diligence, for out of it spring the issues of life.

Proverbs 4:23 (NKJV)

The good man out of the good treasure of his heart produces good, and the evil man out of his evil treasure produces evil; for out of the abundance of the heart his mouth speaks.

Luke 6:45

As in water face reflects face, so a man's heart reveals the man.

Proverbs 27:19 (NKJV)

DISCIPLINE YOUR CHILDREN

A child left undisciplined disgraces its mother.

Proverbs 29:15 (NIV)

He who spares the rod hates his son, but he who loves him is diligent to discipline him.

Proverbs 13:24

Discipline your son, and he will give you rest; he will give delight to your heart.

Proverbs 29:17

GOD IS MERCIFUL

The Lord your God is a merciful God; he will not fail you or destroy you or forget the covenant with your fathers which he swore to them.

Deuteronomy 4:31

But thou, O Lord, art a God merciful and gracious, slow to anger and abounding in steadfast love and faithfulness.

Psalm 86:15

Love your enemies, and do good, and lend, expecting nothing in return; and your reward will be great, and you will be sons of the Most High; for he is kind to the ungrateful and the selfish. Be merciful, even as your Father is merciful.

Luke 6:35–37

COME TO ME

Come to me, all who labor and are heavy laden, and I will give you rest. Take my yoke upon you, and learn from me; for I am gentle and lowly in heart, and you will find rest for your souls. For my yoke is easy, and my burden is light.

Matthew 11:28–30

In the last day, that great day of the feast, Jesus stood and cried, saying, If any man thirst, let him come unto me, and drink.

John 7:37 (KJV)

The Spirit and the Bride say, "Come." And let him who hears say, "Come." And let him who is thirsty come, let him who desires take the water of life without price.

Revelation 22:17

SUBMIT TO GOD

Submit yourselves therefore to God.

James 4:7

They being ignorant of God's righteousness, and going about to establish their own righteousness, have not submitted themselves unto the righteousness of God.

Romans 10:3 (KJV)

Submit yourselves for the Lord's sake to every human authority: whether to the emperor, as the supreme authority, or to governors, who are sent by him to punish those who do wrong and to commend those who do right. For it is God's will that by doing good you should silence the ignorant talk of foolish people.

1 Peter 2:13–15 (NIV)

WATCH YOUR STEP

Watch and pray that you may not enter into temptation; the spirit indeed is willing, but the flesh is weak.

Matthew 26:41

O Lord, I know the way of man is not in himself; it is not in man who walks to direct his own steps.

Jeremiah 10:23 (NKJV)

The steps of a good man are ordered by the Lord, and He delights in his way. Though he fall, he shall not be utterly cast down; for the Lord upholds him with His hand.

Psalm 37:23–24 (NKJV)

DON'T SQUANDER MONEY

Whoever can be trusted with very little can also be trusted with much, and whoever is dishonest with very little will also be dishonest with much. So if you have not been trustworthy in handling worldly wealth, who will trust you with true riches?

Luke 16:10–11 (NIV)

Not many days later, the younger son gathered all he had and took his journey into a far country, and there he squandered his property in loose living.

Luke 15:13

There is desirable treasure, and oil in the dwelling of the wise, but a foolish man squanders it.

Proverbs 21:20 (NKJV)

CHOOSE WORTHY HEROES

Imitate me [Paul], just as I also imitate Christ.

1 Corinthians 11:1 (NKJV)

For though you might have ten thousand instructors in Christ, yet you do not have many fathers; for in Christ Jesus I [Paul] have begotten you through the gospel. Therefore I urge you, imitate me.

1 Corinthians 4:15–16 (NKJV)

We desire each one of you to show the same earnestness in realizing the full assurance of hope until the end, so that you may not be sluggish, but imitators of those who through faith and patience inherit the promises.

Hebrews 6:11–12

BE HIS WITNESS

You shall be my witnesses in Jerusalem and in all Judea and Samaria and to the end of the earth.

Acts 1:8

"You are my witnesses," says the Lord, "and my servant whom I have chosen, that you may know and believe me and understand that I am He. Before me no god was formed, nor shall there be any after me."

Isaiah 43:10

You will be his witness to all people of what you have seen and heard.

Acts 22:15 (NIV)

FOLLOW THE LEADER

[Jesus] called to him the multitude with his disciples, and said to them, "If any man would come after me, let him deny himself and take up his cross and follow me."

Mark 8:34

The Lord is my shepherd, I shall not want; he makes me lie down in green pastures. He leads me beside still waters; he restores my soul. He leads me in paths of righteousness for his name's sake.

Psalm 23:1–3

To this you have been called, because Christ also suffered for you, leaving you an example, that you should follow in his steps.

1 Peter 2:21

HELP THE WIDOW

Religion that God our Father accepts as pure and faultless is this: to look after orphans and widows in their distress and to keep oneself from being polluted by the world.

James 1:27 (NIV)

Learn to do right; seek justice. Defend the oppressed. Take up the cause of the fatherless; plead the case of the widow.

Isaiah 1:17 (NIV)

A father to the fatherless, a defender of widows, is God in his holy dwelling. God sets the lonely in families, he leads out the prisoners with singing; but the rebellious live in a sun-scorched land.

Psalm 68:5–6 (NIV)

ASK FOR HELP

O God, be not far from me; O my God, make haste to help me!

Psalm 71:12

In that day you will ask nothing of me. Truly, truly, I say to you, if you ask anything of the Father, he will give it to you in my name. Hitherto you have asked nothing in my name; ask, and you will receive, that your joy may be full.

John 16:23–24

I lift up my eyes to the hills. From whence does my help come? My help comes from the Lord, who made heaven and earth.

Psalm 121:1–2

CONTROL YOUR APPETITE

When you sit down to eat with a ruler, observe carefully what is before you; and put a knife to your throat if you are a man given to appetite. Do not desire his delicacies, for they are deceptive food.

Proverbs 23:1–3

Keep your eyes on those who live as we do. For, as I have often told you before and now tell you again even with tears, many live as enemies of the cross of Christ. Their destiny is destruction, their god is their stomach, and their glory is in their shame. Their mind is set on earthly things.

Philippians 3:17–19 (NIV)

Add to your faith virtue, to virtue knowledge, to knowledge self-control, to self-control perseverance, to perseverance godliness, to godliness brotherly kindness, and to brotherly kindness love.

2 Peter 1:5–7 (NKJV)

THE ANCHOR HOLDS

We have this hope as an anchor for the soul, firm and secure. It enters the inner sanctuary behind the curtain, where our forerunner, Jesus, has entered on our behalf. He has become a high priest forever, in the order of Melchizedek.

Hebrews 6:19–20 (NIV)

I give them eternal life, and they shall never perish, and no one shall snatch them out of my hand. My Father, who has given them to me, is greater than all, and no one is able to snatch them out of My Father's hand.

John 10:28–29

I have set the Lord always before me: because he is at my right hand, I shall not be moved.

Psalm 16:8 (KJV)

DO NOT OVERSLEEP

A little sleep, a little slumber, a little folding of the hands to sleep—so shall your poverty come on you like a prowler, and your need like an armed man.

Proverbs 6:10–11 (NKJV)

Therefore let us not sleep, as do others; but let us watch and be sober.

1 Thessalonians 5:6 (KJV)

Do not love sleep, or you will grow poor; stay awake and you will have food to spare.

Proverbs 20:13 (NIV)

YOU CAN'T HIDE

Jonah rose to flee to Tarshish from the presence of the Lord. He went down to Joppa, and found a ship going to Tarshish; so he paid the fare, and went on board, to go with them to Tarshish, away from the presence of the Lord.

Jonah 1:3

Where can I go from your Spirit? Where can I flee from your presence? If I go up to the heavens, you are there; if I make my bed in the depths, you are there.

Psalm 139:7–8 (NIV)

Am I a God at hand, says the Lord, and not a God afar off? Can a man hide himself in secret places so that I cannot see him? says the Lord. Do I not fill heaven and earth? says the Lord.

Jeremiah 23:23–24

IT IS FINISHED

Jesus spoke these words, lifted up His eyes to heaven, and said: "Father, the hour has come. Glorify Your Son, that Your Son also may glorify You . . . I have glorified You on the earth. I have finished the work which You have given Me to do."

John 17:1, 4 (NKJV)

Nor was it to offer himself repeatedly, as the high priest enters the Holy Place yearly with blood not his own; for then he would have had to suffer repeatedly since the foundation of the world. But as it is, he has appeared once for all at the end of the age to put away sin by the sacrifice of himself.

Hebrews 9:25–26

When Jesus therefore had received the vinegar, he said, It is finished: and he bowed his head, and gave up the ghost.

John 19:30 (KJV)

Note to the Reader

The publisher invites you to share your response to the message of this book by writing Discovery House Publishers, P.O. Box 3566, Grand Rapids, MI 49501, U.S.A. For information about other Discovery House books, music, videos, or DVDs, contact us at the same address or call 1-800-653-8333. Find us on the Internet at dhp.org or send e-mail to books@dhp.org.